PRAISE FOR *LIFE PRAYERS*

"This delicious collection of prayers is a celebration of wisdom and blessing for all life's passages. The luminous words of comfort, insight, and joy will be a treasured companion that will travel with you through all the bright days and dark nights of the Earthwalk."

—Joan Borysenko, Ph.D.,
author of *Fire in the Soul*

"The most precious gift is that which opens us to life itself. Life Prayers is such a blessing, helping us come alive again—and again—to the wonder of our world, the mystery of our existence, and our solidarity with all beings. This book will be a cherished companion for generations to come."

—Joanna Macy,
author of *World As Lover, World As Self*

"This treasury of wise and loving words is a rich collection of poetry that inspires and teaches us."

—Joan Halifax,
author of *The Fruitful Darkness*

"*Life Prayers* captures the essence of prayer—that universal language through which we unite with each other and the Absolute. The book is spiritual fire. It makes me proud to be a human being."

—Larry Dossey, M.D.,
author of *Healing Words* and *Prayer Is Good Medicine*

LIFE PRAYERS

LIFE PRAYERS

FROM AROUND THE WORLD

365 Prayers, Blessings, and Affirmations
to Celebrate the Human Journey

EDITED BY ELIZABETH ROBERTS & ELIAS AMIDON

HarperSanFrancisco
An Imprint of HarperCollinsPublishers

▓ A TREE CLAUSE BOOK

HarperSanFrancisco and the editors, in association with The Basic Foundation, a not-for-profit organization whose primary mission is reforestation, will facilitate the planting of two trees for every one tree used in the manufacture of this book.

HarperCollins Web Site: http://www.harpercollins.com

HarperCollins®, ▟®, HarperSanFrancisco™, and A TREE CLAUSE BOOK® are trademarks of HarperCollins Publishers Inc.

Illustrations by Kathleen Edwards
Book design by Claudia Smelser
Set in Bembo

Library of Congress Cataloging-in-Publication Data

Life prayers : from around the world : 365 prayers, blessings, and affirmations to celebrate the human journey / edited by Elizabeth Roberts and Elias Amidon. — 1st ed.

Includes bibliographical references and index.

ISBN 0–06–251377–x (pbk.)

1. Prayers. I. Roberts, Elizabeth J. II. Amidon, Elias.

BL560.L49 1996

242'.2—dc20   96–385

01 02 ❖ HAD 10 9 8

This book is dedicated to our friends
Sibylle and Michael Baier.

Your lives are a blessing for all whom you touch.

CONTENTS

Thanks xvii

Prayers for the Human Journey xix

TWO

Kinship with All Life

THREE

The Dark Night of Our Soul

FOUR

Prayers for Solidarity and Justice

Contents

FIVE

Womansprayer

SIX

Initiations

Introduction *179*

Midlife 283

Growing Older 303

SEVEN

Moments of Grace and Illumination

Life Prayers

EIGHT

Earth Praises

THANKS

T HIS BOOK, like all anthologies, belongs foremost to all those whose words grace its pages. We are grateful for their prayers, their insights, and their companionship.

A deep bow of gratitude to the friends, colleagues, teachers, lovers, children, and parents who have inspired the creation of this book—the list is life-long—all those who have gifted our lives with meaning and beauty.

We offer special thanks to Joanna and Fran Macy, Steven Foster and Meredith Little, and Sibylle and Michael Baier. These three couples have been our mentors and friends. Our gratefulness also to Murshida Sitara Brutnell and the wanderers of the Sufi Way for sharing with us the heart of prayer; to Sioux roadman William Baker of the Assemblies of the Morning Star for being "the same all the way through"; to André Patsalides for being always close to That; to Father Thomas Keating for the gift of centering prayer; to John Amidon Velonis for the witness of his faith; and to engaged Buddhists Pracha Hutanuwatr and Sulak Sivaraksa for giving us a chance to practice an earthy spiritual activism.

Many other individuals and organizations have been of special help. Thanks to Tara Strand-Brown and our colleagues from the Institute for Deep Ecology, and to Forrest Ketchin and the team from the Naropa Institute. They gave extra so that we could have the time to finish this book. Thanks also to Mary Rogers for blessing this volume with her knowledge of the Vedas, and to Jac ten Hoeve for spreading the word. Our assistants, Mary Burmaster and Katie Getchell, took on the challenging task of securing permissions—thank you for your patience and warm spirits! The good humor of our agents, Michael Carlisle and Matt Bialer, and the personal commitment of John Loudon, Karen Levine, Mimi Kusch, and Michael Toms of HarperSanFrancisco helped keep the process of creating this book deeply satisfying—thanks.

Last, our gratitude to our children, Jesse, Hanah, Aura, and Aquila, who give us happiness without trying.

PRAYERS FOR THE HUMAN JOURNEY

*"I believe deeply that we must find, all of us together, a new
spirituality. This new concept ought to be elaborated alongside
the religions, in such a way that all people of good will could
adhere to it."*

— *His Holiness the Fourteenth Dalai Lama*

LIFE PRAYERS invites us to partake in the full feast of human life
from birth to death, from despair to celebration, and from solitude to solidarity. In our first book, *Earth Prayers,* we heard the
voices of people from around the world affirming the unity of nature and spirit. The Earth's soul is our own. In *Life Prayers* we see
how this sense of unity can become a potent motivating force in
the world. When we are aware of our place in the larger scheme of
things, daily life becomes more spontaneous and meaningful, and
our actions serve life naturally. We are called beyond an introverted
spirituality to consider everything in our dealings with others as
part of our spiritual life.

After decades of declining influence in the affairs of the world, a
renewal of spirituality is emerging as an antidote to the suffering
of our times. This spiritual renewal is happening both within the
world's great religious traditions and outside of them. It is not

about a specific set of beliefs. As the diverse voices in this volume make clear, the holy Mystery we share appears in many ways—as God, Goddess, Allah, Gaia, Great Spirit, Nirvana. Our human unity transcends this diversity of form and dogma. It is revealing itself in a new ecumenical morality—an all-inclusive Earth ethic. The forces driving this spiritual renewal are twofold: our desire for greater peace of mind and the need for compassionate action.

If these two qualities—peace of mind and compassionate action—are indispensable to the human spiritual journey, the good news is they are also inevitable. However hidden, they are our true nature. They come to life when we practice them. This anthology is a collection of the prayers and poetry of people practicing the virtues of acceptance and compassion, of inner quiet and outer service, of love and action.

Prayer has always been used as a means of cultivating inner peace. Without some measure of equanimity, the spiritual journey is impossible. Prayers offer a skillful means for marrying an inner sense of peace with the outer demands of the world. They help to quiet and focus the agitated mind. They use words to carry us beyond words. As such they are the most primordial language we humans use to align ourselves with the Divine. By silencing inner noise and distractions, prayer brings us into the presence of the moment. Its gift is an inner experience of prayerfulness in which the silent center of life's meaning is revealed.

Prayer also gifts us with a deepening of our compassionate caring for the world. By aligning us with the rest of creation, prayer shows us that the impulse to be of help does not require superior moral fiber or ascetic religious training. It flows naturally out of being human. In serving the common good we learn that we need not become martyrs, sacrificing ourselves in some painful task, but simply become that which we most passionately are.

> First you need only look:
> Notice and honor the radiance of
> Everything about you . . .
> Play in this universe. Tend
> All these shining things around you:
> The smallest plant, the creatures and
> objects in you care.
> Be gentle and nurture. Listen . . .
> As we experience and accept
> All that we really are . . .
> We grow in care.
>
> —Anne Hillman

Of course there are many circumstances that interfere with our quest for peace of mind and compassionate action, events that pressure us to be ambitious, aggressive, or unsympathetic. But the prayers and poems in this book encourage us to look deeply at our reality, to see that we have survived only because of the caring of others. That has been true ever since the cradle. Not only our human family, but the entire Earth family, nourishes us, inspires us and forgives us. We participate in a great web of being that extends through time and space. This is the nature of life on Earth, and in our conscious homecoming to this reality we find peace and compassion.

Many of us are most familiar with traditional prayers of supplication, in which we ask for favors from a God who seems distant from us. In this anthology the emphasis is on prayers that empower, prayers that help us shake loose from our ignorance, attachments, and personal agendas, enabling us to act in concert with the Divine forces already at work. Through life prayer we become co-creators of our world, working in league with a Divine will that is as immediate as our own bodies.

The voices in this book sing out together: "Make of your life an offering! Make of your life a prayer!"

> . . . be awake to the Life
> that is loving you and
> sing your prayer, laugh your prayer,
> dance your prayer, run
> and weep and sweat your prayer,
> sleep your prayer, eat your prayer,
> paint, sculpt, hammer and read your prayer,
> sweep, dig, rake, drive and hoe your prayer,
> garden and farm and build and clean your prayer,
> wash, iron, vacuum, sew, embroider and pickle your prayer,
> compute, touch, bend and fold but never delete
> or mutilate your prayer.
>
> Learn and play your prayer,
> work and rest your prayer,

fast and feast your prayer,
argue, talk, whisper, listen and shout your prayer,
groan and moan and spit and sneeze your prayer,
swim and hunt and cook your prayer,
digest and become your prayer,
release and recover your prayer,
breathe your prayer,
be your prayer.

—Alla Renée Bozarth

PART ONE

Affirmations
and Invocations

After the final no there comes a yes,
And on that yes the future world depends.

—Wallace Stevens

T HE saying of the great Yes! is the root of all life prayers, and so
we begin this book with the prayers of Yes!—with affirmation
and blessing for the furtherance of life. These prayers represent the
most basic and powerful gesture of a heart that has opened to communion with the living world.

The voices in this chapter announce their presence without
fear, and they do so by speaking of what they love (affirmations)
and by calling this forth from the world (invocations). In these
complex and competitive times we may find ourselves feeling that
what we say doesn't matter and that what we do has little effect.
But as the Czech president and playwright Václav Havel reminds
us, "Whether all is really lost or not depends entirely on whether or
not I am lost." Marianne Williamson carries the thought further:

We were born to make manifest
    the glory of God that is within us.
It's not just in some of us;
    it's in everyone.

Affirmations and Invocations

And as we let our own light shine,
  we unconsciously give other people
  permission to do the same.
As we are liberated from our own fear,
  our presence automatically liberates others.

It seems a simple thing, to affirm what we believe. The act of speaking our truth authentically and unsentimentally is a powerful one. It is a gesture of healing for both ourselves and the world we love. Similarly, when we invoke a wish or prayer, what is happening but a process of healing? Even when we wish each other "good day," or, upon parting, catch each other's eyes for a moment and say, "take care," these invocations are our everyday attempt to offer healing to the recipient.

The word *healing* comes from the root "to make whole"—to resolve the inner contradictions within a being and thereby to release its full potential. According to psychologist C. G. Jung, wholeness always includes the sacred dimension, the numinous, and it is at the heart of what it means to be healed. "The approach to the numinous," he wrote, "is the real therapy." Consequently as we affirm and invoke the sacred in our world, we are participating in a great healing.

Many of the prayers in this section of *Life Prayers* are ideally suited to reading aloud with a community or group gathered for a specific purpose. They have the power to align our spirits, inspire us with the deep meaning of our common work, and encourage us to "keep on keeping on" when the going gets rough. Sharing a prayer together in this way touches something in us that other contact and communication rarely does—it allows us to feel our common heart and our common home, and to invoke its wholeness.

> *May the Holy Spirit guide us as we seek to heal and to nurture the earth and all of its creatures, to live in the midst of creation, and to love one another as brothers and sisters with all life.*
>
> —*U.N. Environmental Sabbath*

5

Living Spirits of Earth
Mother and Father of us all
You who hold us in Your breath
You who bathe us in Your waters
who feed us with Your fruits
Guardian of where we are going
of who we are becoming
Cradle of our days
and coffin of our nights
You who carry us folded in Your arms
Sailing silently among the stars
Hear our prayers—

—The Terma Collective

It is I who must begin. . . .

Once I begin, once I try—
here and now,
right where I am,
not excusing myself
by saying that things
would be easier elsewhere,
without grand speeches and
ostentatious gestures,
but all the more persistently
—to live in harmony
with the "voice of Being," as I
understand it within myself
—as soon as I begin that,
I suddenly discover,
to my surprise, that
I am neither the only one,
nor the first,
nor the most important one
to have set out
    upon that road. . . .

Whether all is really lost
or not depends entirely on
whether or not I am lost. . . .

                    —Václav Havel

Affirmations and Invocations

Our deepest fear
    is not that we are inadequate.
Our deepest fear
    is that we are powerful beyond measure.
It is our light,
    not our darkness,
        that most frightens us.
We ask ourselves,
    who am I to be brilliant,
    gorgeous, talented, fabulous?

Actually, who are you not to be?
You are a child of God.
Your playing small doesn't serve the world.
There's nothing enlightened about shrinking
    so that other people
    won't feel insecure around you.

We were born to make manifest
    the glory of God that is within us.
It's not just in some of us;
    it's in everyone.
And as we let our own light shine,
    we unconsciously give other people
    permission to do the same.
As we are liberated from our own fear,
    our presence automatically liberates others.
                —Marianne Williamson

May my feet rest firmly on the ground
May my head touch the sky
May I see clearly
May I have the capacity to listen
May I be free to touch
May my words be true
May my heart and mind be open
May my hands be empty to fill the need
May my arms be open to others
May my gifts be revealed to me
So I may return that which has been given
Completing the great circle.

—The Terma Collective

Empower me
to be a bold participant,
rather than a timid saint in waiting,
in the difficult ordinariness of now;
to exercise the authority of honesty;
rather than to defer to power,
or deceive to get it;
to influence someone for justice,
rather than impress anyone for gain;
and, by grace, to find treasures
of joy, of friendship, of peace
hidden in the fields of the daily
you give me to plow.

—Ted Loder

Affirmations and Invocations

I make the effort
to maintain a ground of oceanic silence
out of which arises the multitude
of phenomena of daily life.

I make the effort
to see and to passionately open in love
to the spirit that infuses all things.

I make the effort
to see the Beloved in everyone
and to serve the Beloved through everyone
(including the earth).

I often fail in these aspirations
because I lose the balance
between separateness and unity,
get lost in my separateness,
and feel afraid.

But I make the effort.

—Ram Dass

I respect the Earth and all living things;
I respect myself.

The ground upon which I walk,
the dirt in which I plant,
the Earth into which I shall return,
is my home.

In returning, I understand that I never left;
it is my emancipation.
Upon seeing, I accept that I am clear light,
it is my salvation.
As I decay, I nurture my Earth, and aid in her preservation.

All things, at once, together and Forever.
Amen.

—Allan Millet

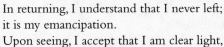

I pledge allegiance to the Earth,
and to the flora, fauna and human life that it supports,
one planet, indivisible,
with safe air, water and soil,
economic justice, equal rights
and peace for all.

—Women's Environment
and Development Organization

Affirmations and Invocations

Offer only lovely things on my altars—
the bread of life, and jewels, and feathers, and flowers.
Let the streams of life flow in peace.
Turn from violence.
Learn to think for a long time how to change this world,
how to make it better to live in.
All the people in the world ought to talk about it
and speak well of it always.
Then it will last forever,
and the flowers will bloom forever,
and I will come to you again.

—Quetzalcoatl

We join with the Earth
and with each other,
to bring new life to the land,
to recreate the human community,
to provide justice and peace,
to remember our children,
to remember who we are. . . .
We join together
as many and diverse expressions
of one loving mystery,
for the healing of the Earth
and the renewal of all Life.

—Pat Cane

The thought manifests as the word;
The word manifests as the deed;
The deed develops into habit;
And habit hardens into character.
    So watch the thought and its ways with care,
And let it spring from love
Born out of concern for all beings.

—The Buddha

Good people,
Most royal greening verdancy,
Rooted in the sun,
You shine with radiant light.
In this circle of earthly existence
You shine so finely,
It surpasses understanding.
God hugs you.
You are encircled by the arms
of the mystery of God.

—Hildegard of Bingen

14

In the beginning, darkness covered the face of the deep.
Then the rushing-breath of life hovered over the waters.
Let us breathe together.
Let us catch our breaths from the need to *make,* to *do.*
Let us be conscious of the Breath of Life.
We breathe out what the trees breathe in.
We breathe in what the trees breathe out.
Together we breathe each other into life.
Blessed is the One within the many.
Blessed are the Many who make one.

—Arthur Waskow

We are all on a journey together . . .
To the center of the universe . . .
Look deep
Into yourself, into another.
It is to a center which is everywhere
That is the holy journey . . .
First you need only look:
Notice and honor the radiance of
Everything about you . . .
Play in this universe. Tend
All these shining things around you:
The smallest plant, the creatures and
objects in your care.
Be gentle and nurture. Listen . . .
As we experience and accept
All that we really are . . .
We grow in care.
We begin to embrace others
As ourselves, and learn to live
As one among many. . . .

—Anne Hillman

First
I thank the Source
of all life
for this life's meaning
then I can begin

first
I create the space
in which to grow
into new dimensions
then I can move there

first
I envision the garden
full of rainbows
and scents of nectar
then I can plant them

first
I touch my heartstring
and feel its resonance
with the harmonics of all
     beings
then I can share love

first
I hear the bird sing
filling the garden
with melodies beyond my ears
then I can appreciate life's
     music

first
I taste the morning light
with which to create
food for my soul
then I can cook
                —Harriet Kofalk

And then all that has divided us will merge
And then compassion will be wedded to power
And then softness will come to a world that is harsh
    and unkind
And then both men and women will be gentle
And then both women and men will be strong
And then no person will be subject to another's will
And then all will be rich and free and varied
And then the greed of some will give way to the needs
    of many
And then all will share equally in the Earth's
    abundance
And then all will care for the sick and the weak
    and the old
And then all will nourish the young
And then all will cherish life's creatures
And then all will live in harmony with each other
    and the Earth
And then everywhere will be called Eden once again
                                    —Judy Chicago

O Great life-giving Spirit
  whose commanding voice I hear in the winds
    and whose warm breath gives life to all the world
Hear me
  one five-billionth of the humans on planet earth.
      I am a natural part of the universe—
        as natural and necessary as the rocks,
          the trees, the birds and the mice
        no more important—nor any less.

Let me walk in beauty
let my spirit see the dynamic spirit of life in all that exists
  with no prejudice or malice toward any creation.
May I begin to remember who I am in the natural order of things
  as I stand in my own shallow pool of time
May I come to know what time it is
  in my life and in all life.

Great Spirit of Love,
Connect my heart to my head
Make me wise
  that I may understand the things you have taught all people.
  in every heart close or far from my own.
Make me courageous when the cold winds of life fall upon me.
Give me strength and endurance for everything that is harsh
  everything that hurts
    everything that makes me squint and wince.

I seek strength not to be greater or lesser than my brother or sister
   but to remove the tough and slimy obstacles to equality
      that have made their home inside myself.
Prepare me to move through life ready to take what comes.
Comfort me and caress me when I am tired and cold.
Unfold me
   the way your gentle breezes unfold the leaves on trees.

Oh Spirit of Creation
   make me always ready to come to you with clean hands
   and straight eyes
      so when life fades as the fading sunset
         my spirit may come to you without shame.
Let me remember every day that the moment will come
   when my sun will go down
   my river will join the vast ocean
   and this rock which has bounced along so many bumps
   will finally come to rest.
Give me a great sky for setting into
   a crystal-clean ocean for flowing into
      and an unpolluted earth for my final resting place.
And when it is time for me to join the earth again
   may I come steadily and with glory.

—Fran Peavey

It's up to us
to re-enchant this planet Earth

We are the elves and giants
we are the shining ones
daughters of the Moon and
sons of the Sun

We are the shapeshifters
we are the mysterious light
shrouded in mists at
the dawn of our time
and it's up to us to re-enchant
this living planet Earth

Up to us to midwife
    at our own rebirth
up to us to send our dead
    along their
ancient pathways to the future
up to us to re-enchant this
living planet Earth

It's up to us to break the spell
that steals the colors
    from the world
and leaves it lifeless
it was our spell
we can break it

It's up to us the break the spell
that steals the music from
the Wind and Rain
it is our spell
we can break it

We will dance the magic dance
and our bodies will remember
we will sing the magic songs
and together we'll remember
how to live together
how to love each other
how to ride the eagle
how to call the deer
Home
        —Will Ashe Bacon

Now is the time,
To climb up the mountain
And reason against habit,
Now is the time.

Now is the time,
to renew the barren soil of nature
Ruined by the winds of tyranny,
Now is the time.

Now is the time,
To commence the litany of hope,
Now is the time. . . .

Now is the time,
To give me roses, not to keep them
For my grave to come,
Give them to me while my heart beats,
Give them today
While my heart yearns for jubilee,
Now is the time. . . .

　　　　　　　　　　—Mzwakhe Mbuli

Help us to harness
the wind,
the water,
the sun,
and all the ready
and renewable
sources of power.

Teach us to conserve,
preserve,
use wisely
the blessed treasures
of our wealth-stored earth.

Help us to share
your bounty
not to waste it,
or pervert it
into peril
for our children
or our neighbors
in other nations.

You who are life
and energy
and blessing,
teach us to revere
and respect
your tender world.
—Thomas John Carlisle

Earth, in which lie the sea, the river, and other waters,
in which food and cornfields have come to be,
in which lives all that breathes and that moves,
may she confer on us the finest of her yield.

Earth, in which the waters, common to all,
moving on all sides, flow unfailingly, day and night,
may she pour us milk in many streams,
and endow us with luster.

May those born of thee, O Earth,
be for our welfare, free from sickness and waste.
Wakeful through a long life, we shall become
bearers of tribute to thee.

Earth, my mother, set me securely with bliss
in full accord with heaven
O wise one,
uphold me in grace and splendor.

—Atharva Veda

Grant what we need each day in bread and insight:
subsistence for the call of
growing life.

Give us the food we need to grow
through each new day,
through each illumination of life's needs.

Let the measure of our need be earthiness:
give all things simple, verdant,
passionate.

Produce in us, for us, the possible:
each only-human step toward home
lit up.

Help us fulfill what lies within
the circle of our lives: each day we ask
no more, no less.

Animate the earth within us: we then
feel the Wisdom underneath
supporting all.

Generate through us the bread of life:
we hold only what is asked to feed
the next mouth.

Grant what we need each day in bread and insight.
—Neil Douglas-Klotz

Abba, Father, we thank you for your presence among us.
Gaia, Mother Earth, we thank you for sustaining us as we go out
   to do the work our faith calls us to do.

We celebrate all the family of creation, heaven and earth, as one
   seamless garment, of which we, too, are an integral part.
We celebrate the soils, which nurture the food for our bodies.
We celebrate the seas, the air, the forests and mountains, which
   nurture our souls.

As a part of all creation, we too have a nurturing role to play.
We have been blessed with the ability to choose our role.
Now in community, we dedicate ourselves to choosing wisely.
Together with the Holy Spirit, we will choose life, that we and our
   children might live.

May the Holy Spirit guide us as we seek to heal and to nurture
   the earth and all of its creatures, to live in the midst of creation,
   and to love one another as brothers and sisters with all life.
And may we travel from this moment forward in awareness of our
   bonds to one another and to the Earth, and in commitment to
   our communities
   wherever they might be.
                              —U.N. Environmental Sabbath

Love all Creation
The whole of it and every grain of sand
Love every leaf
Every ray of God's light
Love the animals
Love the plants
Love everything
If you love everything
You will perceive
The divine mystery in things
And once you have perceived it
You will begin to comprehend it ceaselessly
More and more everyday
And you will at last come to love the whole world
With an abiding universal love

—Fyodor Dostoyevsky

I am at home in the universe. I carry my home with me. No matter where I go, I cannot be less than at home. The forests are the rooms of the house of my childhood. The winds are my mother's arms. The sun is my child's laughter. The caterpillar crawling on my hand is my brother's arm thrown over my shoulder.

The children playing in the street of another country are my children. The stranger's bed encloses me in the sleep of my covers. The earth is my home & its creatures are my family. There is no loneliness to overtake me. I am not stricken to find my home. I breathe interstellar space. The world is pasture for my mind, forage for my imagination. The universe is at home in my mind, its creatures live friendly within me. I live warm and friendly with my fellows in the starry world.

—Ken Patton

Our Mother, whose body is the Earth,
Sacred is thy being. Thy gardens grow.
Thy will be done in our cities,
as it is in nature.
Thanks be this day
for food, and air, and water.
Forgive us our sins against Earth,
as we are learning to forgive one another.
And surrender us not unto extinction,
but deliver us from our folly.
For thine is the beauty, and the power,
and all life, from birth to death,
from beginning to end. Amen.
So be it.
Forever.
Blessed be.

—Henry Horton

May every creature abound in well-being and peace.
May every living being, weak or strong, the long and the small
The short and the medium-sized, the mean and the great
May every living being, seen or unseen, those dwelling far off,
Those near by, those already born, those waiting to be born
May all attain inward peace.

Let no one deceive another
Let no one despise another in any situation
Let no one, from antipathy or hatred, wish evil to anyone at all.
Just as a mother, with her own life,
    protects her only son from hurt
So within yourself foster a limitless concern
    for every living creature.
Display a heart of boundless love for all the world
In all its height and depth and broad extent
Love unrestrained, without hate or enmity.
Then as you stand or walk, sit or lie,
    until overcome by drowsiness
Devote your mind entirely to this,
    it is known as living here life divine.

                                        —The Buddha

May I be peaceful, happy, and light in body and in mind.
May I be safe and free from accidents.
May I be free from anger, unwholesome states of mind, fear,
    and worries.
May I know how to look at myself with the eyes of
    understanding and love.
May I be able to recognize and touch the seeds of joy
    and happiness in myself.
May I learn how to nourish myself with joy each day.
May I be able to live fresh, solid, and free.
May I not fall into the state of indifference
or be caught in the extremes of attachment and aversion.

May you be peaceful, happy, and light in body and mind.
May you be safe and free from accidents.
May you be free from anger, unwholesome states of mind, fear
    and worries.
May you know how to look at yourself with the eyes of
    understanding and love.
May you be able to recognize and touch the seeds of joy
    and happiness in yourself.
May you learn how to nourish yourself with joy each day.
May you be able to live fresh, solid, and free.
May you not fall into the state of indifference
or be caught in the extremes of attachment and aversion.

May all beings be peaceful, happy, and light in body and mind.
May all beings be safe and free from accidents.
May all beings be free from anger, unwholesome states of mind,
   fear, and worries.
May all beings know how to look at themselves with the eyes
   of understanding and love.
May all beings be able to recognize and touch the seeds
   of joy and happiness in themselves.
May all beings learn how to nourish themselves with joy each day.
May all beings be able to live fresh, solid, and free.
May all beings not fall into the state of indifference
or caught in the extremes of attachment and aversion.

—Thich Nhat Hanh

I have no parents
    I make the heaven and earth my parents
I have no home
    I make awareness my home
I have no life and death
    I make the tides of breathing my life and death
I have no divine powers
    I make honesty my divine power
I have no means
    I make understanding my means
I have no secrets
    I make my character my secret
I have no body
    I make endurance my body
I have no eyes
    I make the flash of lightning my eyes
I have no ears
    I make sensibility my ears
I have no limbs
    I make promptness my limbs

I have no miracles
   I make right action my miracle
I have no principles
   I make adaptability to all circumstances my principle
I have no tactics
   I make emptiness and fullness my tactics
I have no talent
   I make ready wit my talent
I have no friends
   I make my mind my friend
I have no enemy
   I make carelessness my enemy
I have no armor
   I make benevolence and righteousness my armor
I have no castle
   I make immovable mind my castle
I have no sword
   I make absence of self my sword
                    —Samurai song (fifteenth century)

We call first on the Beings of the Past. Be with us now all you who have gone before, you our ancestors and teachers. You who walked and loved and faithfully tended this Earth be present to us now that we may carry on the legacy you bequeathed us. Aloud and silently in our hearts we say your names and see your faces. . . .

We call also on the Beings of the Present: All you with whom we live and work on this endangered planet, all you with whom we share this brink of time, be with us now. Fellow humans and brothers and sisters of other species, help us open to our collective will and wisdom. Aloud and silently we say your names and picture your faces. . . .

Lastly, we call on the Beings of the Future. All you who will come after us on this Earth, be with us now. All you who are waiting to be born in the ages to come, it is for your sakes too, that we work to heal our world. We cannot picture your faces or say your names—you have none yet—but we would feel the reality of your claim on life. It helps us to be faithful in the task that must be done, so that there will be for you, as there was for our ancestors, blue sky, fruitful land, clear waters.

—Joanna Macy

In the next century
or the one beyond that
they say,
are valleys, pastures.
We can meet there in peace
if we make it.
To climb these coming crests
one word to you, to
you and your children:
stay together
learn the flowers
go light

—Gary Snyder

Who shall ascend into the hill of the Lord? or who
shall stand in his holy place? There is no one but us.
There is no one to send, nor a clean hand, nor a pure
heart on the face of the earth, nor in the earth, but
only us, a generation comforting ourselves with the
notion that we have come at an awkward time, that
our innocent fathers are all dead—as if innocence had
ever been—and our children busy and troubled, and
we ourselves unfit, not yet ready, having each of us
chosen wrongly, made a false start, failed, yielded to
impulse and the tangled comfort of pleasures, and
grown exhausted, unable to seek the thread, weak, and
involved. But there is no one but us. There never has
been.

—Annie Dillard

The first thing
The last thing.
Start from where you are.

—Dale Pendell

PART TWO

Kinship
with All Life

THERE is a longing in us to return to our native place, to meet once again with our kin in the Earth community. We are being called home to a wider world of life, of wilderness and spontaneity, the world of wind and rain, of oak and maple and pineland forests, of the eagle and the chickadee, the wolf and the bear, and the many other beings—all our relations—with whom we share this Earth. Though ours is a time of increasing habitat destruction, species extinction, and sprawling concrete metropolises, more and more people are seeking companionship and meaning beyond the boundaries of humanity. We begin to remember our larger family and we find they have remained loyal to our ancient bond.

To our ancestors, the visitation of animals or the simple sound of the wind in the trees carried messages from the Creator and the spirits of Earth. The entire landscape was known to be sacred and infused with creativity, meaning, and its own evolutionary story. Physically and spiritually we are woven into this story. Yet today it seems that the manifestations of nature are noticed almost entirely for their market value. We have chased the gods from the groves, and nature is owned and traded as a stock of "resources" for our use. We human animals are left to suffer a loneliness the source of which we may not even remember.

Kinship with All Life

If we pretend
that we are at the center,
that moles and kingfishers,
eels and coyotes
are at the edge of grace,
then we circle, dead moons
about a cold sun.

—Joseph Bruchac

The prayers of kinship in this chapter speak to us of a way back from this alienation. Many of the voices are Native American or have been deeply influenced by Native American insight. It is a humbling and powerful lesson to realize that after all the European colonists destroyed of native cultures and natural habitat, this deep gift of affiliation and belonging is so beautifully offered to the descendants of the invaders. These voices speak of a renewed courtesy toward the Earth and all of its inhabitants. They remind us that only by sensing our relationships with the four-legged and the winged ones, with rocks and rivers and green things, can we maintain the richness of our own lives. Our perceptions of our selves, the expressions of our imaginations, and even our intimations of the Divine are all reliant upon our understanding of our connectedness to other creatures.

Earth mother teach me of my kin,
Of Hawk and dove and flower,
Of blinding sunlight, shady knoll,
desert wind and morning showers.

Teach me every language of
the creatures that sing to me,
That I may count the cadence of
Infinite lessons in harmony.

—Jamie Sams

Through these prayers we are able to speak and listen in new ways—because in prayer we are not just talking to ourselves, but admitting another presence. By entering into openhearted dialogue with this "other," we are sometimes able to hear our truest voices speak back to us clearly, telling us about a life greater than our own. As you read these prayers you will see that whenever we are properly humble and willing to let something besides a human be our teacher, the Earth's creatures share priceless wisdom with us.

Let my words
be bright with animals,
images the flash of a gull's wing.
If we pretend
that we are at the center,
that moles and kingfishers,
eels and coyotes
are at the edge of grace,
then we circle, dead moons
about a cold sun.
This morning I ask only
the blessing of the crayfish,
the beatitude of the birds;
to wear the skin of the bear
in my songs;
to work like a man with my hands.
　　　　　　　　　—Joseph Bruchac

Hear me, four quarters of the world—a relative I am!
Give me the strength to walk the soft earth,
    a relative to all that is!
Give me the eyes to see and the strength to understand
    that I may be like you . . .
Great Spirit, Great Spirit, my Grandfather,
all over the earth the faces of living things are all alike.
With tenderness have these come up out of the ground.
Look upon these faces of children without number
    and with children in their arms
that they may face the winds and walk the good road
    to the day of quiet.

—Black Elk

43

Pray for the animals, you that pray, you that beg for mercy,
for success and for peace,
the immanent spirit has also been poured into them,
they are also souls, more complete than you,
and clear, brave, beautiful;

and if we begin from the beginning, who knows,
we shall have to share also these sufferings,
simpler, more severe, more unlimited than ours.

—Eeva-Liisa Manner

O God, scatterer of ignorance and darkness,
    grant me your strength.
May all beings regard me with the eye of a friend,
    and I all beings!
With the eye of a friend may each single being
    regard all others!

—Yojht Veda, XXXVI, 18

Earth Mother teach me of my kin,
Of Hawk, and Dove, and flower,
Of blinding sunlight, shady knoll,
Desert wind and morning showers.
Teach me every language of
The creatures that sing to me,
That I may count the cadence of
Infinite lessons in harmony.
Teach me how to honor
The Sacred Spaces of all,
Gently melding with the whole,
Answering the whippoorwill's call.
Steamy tropics to glacial ice,
To thundering ocean tides,
In every grain of desert sands,
Your beauty forever abides.
Oh, Mother of every kingdom,
Let me claim my family's love,
From the whales of the deepest oceans,
To the Winged-ones, high above.
Expand my limited vision
Until I can truly know
The missions of my Relations
And the blessings they bestow.

—Jamie Sams

Blessed are the animals
For they shall lead us back
To our lost innocence.

Blessed are the great whales
For their vast intelligence
Is peaceful.

Blessed is the wolf
For he was there
At the dawn of Creation.

Blessed is the eagle
For he is the king of birds.

Blessed are the pigeon and the sparrow
For their willingness to live with us.

Blessed is the cow
For she is the ancient symbol of Peace.

Blessed is the little mouse
Who seeks shelter from the cold.

Blessed are the otters
For their playfulness
Is without guile.

Blessed are the bees
For they make Earth
Fruitful and green.

Blessed are our cousins
The Great Apes

Who we have abused
Unmercifully.

Blessed are the elephants
For they are pure of heart.

Blessed are the pigs
For their suffering is unsurpassed.

Blessed are the great cats
For surely their perfection
Has no equal.

Blessed are all wild, free things
For they live in harmony
With their Mother.

Blessed are those animals
Who are part of our families
For they bind us to the rest of Creation.
And blessed be Humankind
Who has gone so far astray.

May we listen to Earth's other voices
And become shepherds to the flock.

Blessed is the Creation
In its magnificence.
For the Spirit dwells
In every living thing.

And is indivisible.

—Mary de La Valette

Sometimes, loping along, I almost find
that band of sorrow the wolves found. Long nights
they steal forth where moonlight follows their breath;
they bring their faces near and let the whining
begin: it strings puppy and wolf together.
That long pang across the horizon tells
how a hunter called Man will come. In the night by a fire
their guttural plan will blaze. A banner of woe,
the wolf cry goes in the wind, lifting their moan.

Now they are almost extinguished. Their tendered song
has melted into The North, where trees and stones
wait for our song, when we meet in the cold
with our faces near and begin our low whine
that means we are on the trail the wolves have gone.
                                                    —William Stafford

In the name of Raven. In the name of Wolf. In the name of Whale. In the name of Snake. Who have taught us. Who have guided us. Who have sustained us. Who have healed us.

Please heal the animals.

In the name of Raven. In the name of Wolf. In the name of Whale. In the name of Snake. Whom we have slaughtered. Whom we have feared. Whom we have caged. Whom we have persecuted. Whom we have slandered. Whom we have cursed. Whom we have tortured.

Please protect the animals.

In the name of Raven. In the name of Wolf. In the name of Whale. In the name of Snake. Whose habitat we have stolen. Whose territory we have plundered. Whose feeding grounds we have paved and netted. Whose domain we have poisoned. Whose food we have appropriated. Whose young we have killed. Whose lives and ways of life we have threatened.

Please restore the animals.

In the name of Raven. In the name of Wolf. In the name of Whale. In the name of Snake.
Forgive us. Have mercy. May the animals return. Not as a resurrection but as living beings. On earth.

On this earth that is also theirs.

Oh Great Spirit. Please heal the animals. Please protect the animals. Please restore the animals.

So our lives may also be healed. So our souls may be protected. So our spirits may be restored.

Oh Spirit of Raven. Oh Spirit of Wolf. Oh Spirit of Whale. Oh Spirit of Snake.

Teach us, again, how to live.

—Deena Metzger

50

I ask sometimes why these small animals
With bitter eyes, why we should care for them.

I question the sky, the serene blue water,
But it cannot say. It gives no answer.

And no answer releases in my head
A procession of grey shades patched and whimpering.

Dogs with clipped ears, wheezing cart horses
A fly without shadow and without thought.

51

Is it with these menaces to our vision
With this procession led by a man carrying wood

We must be concerned? The holy land, the rearing
Green island should be kindlier than this.

Yet the animals, our ghosts, need tending to.
Take in the whipped cat and blinded owl;

Take up the man-trapped squirrel upon your shoulder.
Attend to the unnecessary beasts.

From growing mercy and a moderate love
Great love for the human animal occurs.

And your love grows. Your great love grows
　　and grows.

—Jon Silkin

To pray you open your whole self
To sky, to earth, to sun, to moon
To one whole voice that is you
And know there is more
That you can't see, can't hear
Can't know except in moments
Steadily growing, and in languages
That aren't always sound but other
Circles of motion
Like eagle that Sunday morning
Over Salt River. Circled in blue sky
In wind, swept our hearts clean
With sacred wings.
We see you, see ourselves and know
That we must take the utmost care
And kindness in all things.
Breathe in, knowing we are made of
All this, and breathe, knowing
We are truly blessed because we
Were born, and die soon, within a
True circle of motion,
Like eagle rounding out the morning
Inside us.
We pray that it will be done
In beauty.
In beauty.

—Joy Harjo

I pray to the birds.
I pray to the birds because I believe
   they will carry the messages of my heart upward.
I pray to them because I believe in their existence,
the way their songs begin and end each day
   —the invocations and benedictions of earth.
I pray to the birds because they remind me of what I love
   rather than what I fear.
And at the end of my prayers,
   they teach me how to listen.

> —Terry Tempest Williams

An eagle is walking,
Toward me it is walking.
Its long feathers blow in the breeze.

A hawk is running,
Toward me it is running.
Its down feathers ruffle in the wind.

> —Papago song

They lived high on a hill.
They were people who were up before
first light.
They did not have peculiar customs.
They would not bother anybody.

They were of the following minds—
    crows, hawks, horned owls
    field larks, hummingbirds
    blue birds, chickadees
    quails, woodpeckers
    yellow hammers, whippoorwills.

They did not work, they lived easy.
The best of them were wiser
than other clans.
They did not depend on anyone
but themselves.

They were the Bird Clan.

—Chickasaw song

There is craft in this smallest insect,
With strands of web spinning out his thoughts;
In his tiny body finding rest,
And with the wind lightly turning.
Before the eaves he stakes out his broad earth;
For a moment on the fence top lives through his life.
When you know that all beings are even thus,
You will know what creation is made of.

—Sugaware no Michizane

The water bug
is drawing
the shadows of the evening
toward him on the water.

—Yaqui song

We bless you, cicada,
high in the branches.
You sip a dew drop
and whistle like a king.
What you see is yours:
all the soft meadows
and furry mountains.
Yet you do no harm
in the farmer's field,
and men exalt you
as the voice of summer.
You are loved by Muses
and Apollo himself
who gave you clear song.
Wise child of the earth,
old age doesn't waste you.
Unfeeling and bloodless
you are like a god.

—Anakreon (ca. 560 B.C.)

Welcome, o Supernatural One, o Swimmer,
who returns every year in this world
that we may live rightly, that we may be well.
I offer you, swimming salmon, my heart's deep gratitude.

I ask that you will come again,
that next year we will meet in this life,
that you will see that nothing evil should befall me.
O Supernatural One, o Swimmer,
now I will do to you what you came here for me to do.
                              —Kwakiutl Women's prayer

I say the blessing of Brighid
That she placed about her calf and her cows,
About her horses and her goats,
About her sheep and her lambs:

Each day and night
In cold and heat
Each day and night,
In light and darkness:

Keep them from marsh,
Keep them from rocks,
Keep them from pits,
Keep them from banks;

Keep them from harm,
Keep them from jealousy,
Keep them from spell,
Keep North to South;

Keep them from poison,
From East and West,
Keep them from envy,
And from all harmful intentions.

—Carmina Gadelica

Now sleep the mountain peaks and ravines,
ridges and torrent streams, all creeping things
that black night nourishes,
wild upland beasts and the race of bees,
and monsters in the gulfs of the dark-gleaming
sea; now sleep the tribes of long-winged birds.
                              —Alcman (seventh century B.C.)

The least little sound sets the coyote walking,
walking the edge of our comfortable earth.
We look inward, but all of them
are looking toward us as they walk the earth.

We need to let animals loose in our houses,
the wolf to escape with a pan in his teeth,
and streams of animals toward the horizon
racing with something silent in each mouth.

For all we have taken into our keeping
and polished with our hands belongs to a truth
greater than ours, in the animals' keeping.
Coyotes are circling around our truth.
                              —William Stafford

Kinship with All Life

Plants and Animals in the Garden,
We welcome you—we invite you in—
we ask your forgiveness and your understanding.
Listen as we invoke your names, as we also listen for you:
Little sparrows, quail, robins, and house finches
    who have died in our strawberry nets;
Young Cooper's hawk who flew into our sweet pea trellis
    and broke your neck;
Numerous orange-bellied newts who died in our shears,
    in our irrigation pipes, by our cars, and by our feet;
Gophers and moles, trapped and scorned by us,
    and also watched with love, admiration, and awe
    for your one-mindedness;
And all plants we have shunned: poison hemlock, pigweed,
bindweed, stinging nettle, bull thistle;
We call up plants we have removed by dividing you
    and separating you, and by deciding
    you no longer grow well here.
We invoke you and thank you and continue to learn from you.
We dedicate this ceremony to you.
We will continue to practice with you and for you.
                                —Green Gulch Zen Center

60

I send prayers of gratitude to all
that has given of itself on this day.
The strong beans, and the hardy grains,
the beautiful leafy green plants and the sweet juicy fruits.
I thank the sun that warmed and vitalized them,
   just as it does me,
and the earth that held and nourished them, as it does me,
and the waters that bathed and refreshed them, as they do for me.
I thank the fire that transformed them,
just as I wish to be transformed by the fires of Spirit.
I thank the hands that grew and prepared this food,
just as I thank all those that have touched me in so many ways.
—Sedonia Cahill

On mountains, by rivers, in valleys,
in hidden recesses,
there grow the plants, trees, and herbs;
trees, both great and small,
the shoots of the ripening grain,
grape vine and sugar cane.
Fertilized are these by the rain
and abundantly enriched;
the dry ground is soaked;
herbs and trees flourish together.
From the one water which issued from the clouds,
plants, trees, thickets, forests,
according to need receive moisture.
All the various trees, lofty, medium, low,
each according to its size,
grow and develop roots, stalks, branches, leaves,
blossoms and fruits in their brilliant colors;
wherever the one rain reaches,
all become fresh and glossy.
According as their bodies, forms, and natures
are great and small,
so the enriching rain,
though it is one and the same,
yet makes each of them flourish.

—The Lotus Sutra

Silently a flower blooms,
    In silence it falls away;
Yet here now, at this moment, at this place,
    The world of the flower, the whole of
    the world is blooming.
This is the talk of the flower, the truth
    of the blossom;
    The glory of eternal life is fully shining here.
          —Zenkei Shibayama

63

The forest is one big thing;
it has people, animals, plants.
There is no point in saving the forests
if the forest is burned down;
there is no point saving the forest
if the people and animals who live in it
are killed or driven away.
The groups trying to save the animals
cannot win if the people trying to save the forest lose;
the people trying to save the Indians cannot win
if either of the others loses . . .
          —Paiakan

Our Father, we thank Thee for Trees!
We thank Thee for the trees of our childhood
in whose shade we played and read and dreamed;
for the trees of our schooldays,
the trees along the paths where friendship walked.
We thank Thee for special trees
which will always stand large in our memory
because for some reason of our own they became our trees.
We thank Thee for the great stretches of trees
which make the forests.
May we always stand humbly before Thy trees
and draw strength from them as they, in their turn,
draw sustenance from Thy bounties of earth and sun and air.
—Margueritte Harmon Bro

64

Outside my window
two tall witch-elms
toss their inspired
green heads in the sun
and lean together
whispering.

Trees make the world
a proper place.

—Robert Nye

Yesterday I became mindful of you.
It happened when I saw you
burning for us in the fireplace,
giving us everything you had.
There would be nothing left but ashes
that would fertilize the earth.
You appear as lumber, popsicle sticks, firewood,
furniture, toothpicks, and paper.
You do these things for us without protest.

65

But you also live for the birds,
squirrels, grubs, and the wind.
You hold the soil in place
and provide clean water.
You make the air new each day,
and startle us with shapes and colors,
as beautiful naked in the winter
as clothed in the summer.

What do we do for you?
Now, we don't even stay out of your way.
We don't honor your community, your home.

Yet even as a stump,
you're proud to host our Buddha shrine.
You show us unconditional love.

—Bill Clarke

Lord, it may seem odd
That I should pray here, now.
But when I plant trees
I've things to say to God.

These little trees are Yours,
You know, not just mine.
A redwood grove twelve inches
    tall
Is hardly anyone's at all,
I suppose, except by faith.

A man gets to wondering,
Between bulldozers and the
    fears
Of war, why look ahead
A hundred, even thirty years?

I don't know . . . except
As these trees grow
I hope my great grandchildren
Or someone's boys and girls
Play hide-and-seek
Among the towering trunks
And chattering squirrels.

I hope they hear beauty
In the singing boughs
And birds. I hope they
Breathe clean forest air
And find Your peace.

When my hands press moist
    soil
Carefully about the roots
I feel Your life and love,
I feel a world reborn.

O, God, heal the scars
Of earth with trees,
And not with snags
and thorn.
            —Arthur O. Roberts

I am a stag: *of seven tines,*
I am a flood: *across a plain,*
I am a wind: *on a deep lake,*
I am a tear: *the Sun lets fall,*
I am a hawk: *above the cliff,*
I am a thorn: *beneath the nail,*
I am a wonder: *among flowers,*
I am a wizard: *who but I*
Sets the cool head aflame with smoke?

I am a spear: *that roars for blood,*
I am a salmon: *in a pool,*
I am a lure: *from paradise,*
I am a hill: *where poets walk,*
I am a boar: *ruthless and red,*
I am a breaker: *threatening doom,*
I am a tide: *that drags to death,*
I am an infant: *who but I*
Peeps from the unhewn dolmen arch?

I am the womb: *of every holt,*
I am the blaze: *on every hill,*
I am the queen: *of every hive,*
I am the shield: *for every head,*
I am the tomb: *of every hope.*

—Amergin's Charm
(translated by Robert Graves)

And when, Humanity, you will return to Nature, on that day your eyes will open, you will gaze straight into the eyes of Nature, and in its mirror you will see your own image. You will know that you have returned to yourself, that when you hid from Nature, you hid from yourself. When you return you will see that from you, from your hands and from your feet, from your body and from your soul, heavy, hard, oppressive fragments will fall and you will stand erect. You will understand that these were fragments of the shell into which you had shrunk in the bewilderment of your heart, and out of which you had finally emerged. On that day you will know that your former life did not befit you, that you must renew all things, your food, your drink, your dress and your home, your manner of work, and your mode of study—everything! On that day, deep in your heart, you will know that you had been wandering until you returned to Nature. For you did not know life. A different life, a life not ready-made, a life to be experienced in preparation and creation—that life you did not know. Therefore your life was cut in two—a very small shred of existence and a huge experience of non-existence, of work, of labor, of busy-ness. You did not think, and it did not occur to you, that there is no life in a life ready-made. Preparation is itself Life, for Nature also lives within the preparation of life, within the creation of life.

—A. D. Gordon

We need the tonic of wilderness, to wade sometimes in marshes where the bittern and the meadow-hen lurk, and hear the booming of the snipe; to smell the whispering sedge where only some wilder and more solitary fowl builds her nest, and the mink crawls with its belly close to the ground.

At the same time that we are earnest to explore and learn all things, we require that all things be mysterious and unexplorable, that land & sea be infinitely wild, unsurveyed and unfathomed by us because unfathomable.

We can never have enough of nature. We must be refreshed by the sight of inexhaustible vigor, vast and titanic features, the sea-coast with its wrecks, the wilderness with its living and its decaying trees, the thundercloud, and the rain which lasts three weeks and produced freshets. We need to witness our own limits transgressed, and some life pasturing freely where we never wander.

—Henry David Thoreau

Stand still. The trees ahead and the bushes beside you
Are not lost. Where ever you are is called HERE.
And you must treat it as a powerful stranger.
Must ask permission to know it and be known.
The forest breathes. Listen. It answers,
I have made this place around you.
If you leave it, you may come back again, saying, HERE.
No two trees are the same to Raven.
No two branches are the same to wren.
If what a tree or bush does is lost on you,
You are surely lost. Stand still. The forest knows
Where you are. You must let it find you.

—David Wagoner

PART THREE

The Dark Night
of Our Soul

NOTHING in the history of humanity has prepared us for what our generation is now living through. We hear phrases such as "the death of Nature" or the need to "save the planet." But by using such sweeping terms we may be avoiding the deeper truth. It is not the Earth or nature that will die—the vast forces that create and maintain life will certainly survive our carelessness—it is a loss much closer to ourselves and to our souls. In our pursuit of material "progress" and consumer products, we are compromising the quality and meaning of our lives and the future of many members of the Earth community. It has been said that during the next fifty years one quarter of the Earth's life forms will become extinct. With the loss of each species we are losing a mode of Divine revelation that will never appear again.

Beneath this reality lies a great despair. Human civilization itself is going through a dark night of the soul.

> It is the destruction of the world
> in our own lives that drives us
> half insane, and more than half.
> To destroy that which we were given
> in trust: how shall we bear it?
>
> —Wendell Berry

The Dark Night of Our Soul

As the last of the ancient forests fall, as the topsoil erodes, as the oceans lose their richness, and the air and even the sunlight become toxic, we stand before the miracle of creation, and our sense of awe is eclipsed by our sadness, rage, or shame. To be ashamed before the rest of creation—is that our destiny as a species?

In the first half of this chapter, brave souls speak of this collective pain. Why? they ask. How are we to endure this sad, slow graying of everything beautiful, green, and forgiving? Through these prayers we practice sustaining our gaze at the suffering caused by human actions. We remember the importance of not turning away even when the suffering is in the depths of our own soul.

Human life has always been touched by moments of despair and hopelessness. There comes to many, perhaps all people, a time of inner turmoil and spiritual dryness. The collective grief of our times may cloud our more personal moments of despair, but few of us escape our own dark night of the soul. Prayers of the personal dark night speak from the second half of this chapter, crying out when God cannot be found. In this crucible we are made to wait, unknowing. These are the times when "the struggle just gets tired," when we toss awake all night disheartened by our failures, discouraged by our weakness.

> I know the purity of pure despair,
> My shadow pinned against a sweating wall.
> That place among the rocks—is it a cave,
> Or winding path? The edge is what I have . . .
> —Theodore Roethke

Spiritual teachers and psychologists speak of the wisdom to be gained from traversing the arid terrain of hopelessness. Understanding our "dark night" as a spiritual descent and quest for freedom may offer some assurance in a difficult time. Certainly when despair grows within us it may feel hard to pray, but pray is what we must do. Pray to give voice to our truth. Pray to avoid denial. Pray to remember that we are not the first, nor will we be the last, to know the dark night of the soul. Pray with faith that a miracle will be born not out of our own doing, but from the unconscious depths of our being.

It is the destruction of the world
in our own lives that drives us
half insane, and more than half.
To destroy that which we were given
in trust: how will we bear it?
It is our own bodies that we give
to be broken, our bodies
existing before and after us
in clod and cloud, worm and tree
that we, driving or driven, despise
in our haste to die, our country
spent in shining cars speeding
to junk. To have lost, wantonly,
the ancient forests, the vast grasslands
is our madness, the presence
in our very bodies of our grief.

—Wendell Berry

In our own generation
we tremble on the verge of Flood.

The air is full of poison.
The rain, the seas, are full of poison.
The Earth hides arsenals of poisonous fire,
seeds of light surcharged with fatal darkness.
The ice is melting,
the seas are rising,
the air is dark with smoke and rising heat.

Who speaks for the redwood and the rock, the lion and the
    beetle?
Who are our Noahs?
Who can teach us to be "Restful-ones"?
Where is our Ark?
Who can renew the Rainbow?

What must we do to reaffirm
the covenant between the Breath of Life
and all who live and breathe upon this planet?
                                        —Arthur Waskow

Gracious God,
who made the covenant promise with our ancestors,
we gather here today a rebellious people.
We want to act out your intentions for us,
but we keep getting mixed up
by all the glitter of the world around us.
You tell us to honor creation,
and we use other people and animals and plant life
only to meet our wants.
You offer daily bread to every living creature,
and we steal that bread from our brothers and sisters
in the name of our greed.
You promise us new life,
and we shrink back from it in fear.
Heal us, God, lest we destroy ourselves.
We need your presence among us. Amen.

—U.N. Environmental Sabbath

We have forgotten who we are,
we have lost our sense of wonder and connectedness,
we have degraded the Earth and our fellow creatures,
and we have nowhere else to go.

if we lose the sweetness of the waters,
    we lose the life of the land,
if we lose the life of the land,
    we lose the majesty of the forest,
if we lose the majesty of the forest,
    we lose the purity of the air,
if we lose the purity of the air,
    we lose the creatures of the Earth,

not just for ourselves,
but for our children,
both now and in the future.

—Earth Charter

The great whale you made,
The polar bear, the golden eagle:
See how they die, my Lord, in air and water
Which also once you made. Save water,
Air, save world—remember, Sir,
The days of its creation—save it all,
Beginning now, let no more forms
Perish. For they do, you let them do—
Forgive me—and say nothing. Why,
Lord, do you not rage?
The lion, too, and the leopard—why,
O you that gave them life,
Do you not thunder, halting their destruction?
The steaming hippopotamus, the trumpeting
Elephant: those also, good my Lord,
Are worthy of your wrath. Why, then—
Forgive, forgive me,
But I ask.

—Mark Van Doren

I want to know why
The rain is falling
I want to know why
There is a rainbow in the sky
I want to know why
The people are hungry
Why
Life in this country is at a
    standstill
Why
The days seem to grow longer
And life shorter
Why
The people are forced to
    tighten their belts
Watching their harvest
Being shipped off
Why
Children have no milk on their
    table
Neither rice to eat

I want to know why
Those children are singing
Why
There is a red moon sleeping in
    the sea
Why
Soldiers are trained to kill
To hate
To rage
To savage
To steal
Why darkness is coming
As darkness has
Reigned
For so long . . .
But above all
I want to wake up in the
    morning and hear
Everybody shouting
WHY? WHY? WHY?
       —Helvecio Mendes

God, again and again through the ages you have sent messengers
    To this pitiless world:
They have said, "Forgive everyone," they have said,
    "Love one another—Rid your hearts of evil."
They are revered and remembered, yet still in these dark days
We turn them away with hollow greetings, from outside the doors
    of our houses.

And meanwhile I see secretive hatred murdering the helpless
    Under the cover of night;
And Justice weeping silently and furtively at power misused,
    No hope of redress.
I see young men working themselves into a frenzy,
In agony dashing their heads against stone to no avail.

My voice is choked today; I have no music in my flute:
    Black moonless night
Has imprisoned my world, plunged it into nightmare.
And this is why
    With tears in my eyes, I ask:
Those who have poisoned your air, those who have
    extinguished your light,
Can it be that you have forgiven them? Can it be
    that you love them?

—Rabindranath Tagore

Now in the people
that were meant to be green,
there is no more life of any kind.
There is only shrivelled barrenness.

The winds are burdened
by the utterly awful stink of evil,
selfish goings-on.

Thunderstorms menace.
The air belches out
the filthy uncleanliness of the peoples.

There pours forth an unnatural,
a loathsome darkness,
that withers the green,
and wizens the fruit
that was to serve as food for the people.

Sometimes this layer of air
is full,
full of a fog that is the source
of many destructive and barren creatures,
that destroy and damage the earth,
rendering it incapable
of sustaining humanity.

—Hildegard of Bingen

God signs to us
    we cannot read
She shouts
    we take cover
She shrugs
    and trains leave
        the tracks

Our schedules! we moan
Our loved ones

God is fed up
All the oceans she gave us
All the fields
All the acres of steep seedful forests
And we did what
    Invented the Great Chain
        of Being and
    the chain saw
    Invented sin

God sees us now
    gorging ourselves &
    starving our neighbors
    starving ourselves &
    storing our grain
& She says

I've had it
    you cast your trash
    upon the waters—
    it's rolling in

    You stuck your fine fine finger
    into the mystery of life
        to find death

    & you did
    you learned how to end
    the world
    in nothing flat

Now you come crying
    to your mommy
Send us a miracle
Prove that you exist

Look at your hand, I say
Listen to your sacred heart
Do you have to haul the tide in
sweeten the berries on the vine

I set you down
a miracle among miracles
You want more
It's your turn
You show me

85

                                    —George Ella Lyon

The children of God are homeless.
They are hungry and wander like specters;
they are thirsty and find no shade for their sun.
Above them are the small, human gods—
the tyrants
whose uproar breaks the harmony
of the wind.
Plant the deserts with wheat,
fill the seas with fresh water,
calm the wrath of God:
The one who built the world
can destroy it.

—Maria Teresa Sanchez

God hoped for justice,
But behold, injustice;
For equity,
But behold, iniquity!
Woe to those who add house to house
And join field to field,
Till there is room for none but you
To dwell in the land!

—Isaiah 5:7–8

Weep, my unfortunate people!
  All this you will see take place.
Weep, my unfortunate people!
  For the waters will overwhelm the land.
Weep, my unhappy relatives!
  You will learn all.
Weep, my unfortunate relatives!
  You will learn all.
The waters will overwhelm the mountains.

—Pima song

. . . I feel the age we live in is drawing to a close—
    Upheavals threaten, gather the pace
        Of a storm that nothing slows.

Hatred and envy swell to violent conflagration:
    Panic spreads down from the skies,
        From their growing devastation.

If nowhere in the sky is there left a place
    For the gods to be seated, then, Indra,
        Thunderer, may you place

At the end of this history your direst instruction:
    A last full stop written in the fire
        Of furious total destruction.

Hear the prayer of an earth that is stricken with pain:
    In the green woods, O may the birds
        Sing supreme again.

                —Rabindranath Tagore

Search. Search. Seek. Seek.
Cold. Cold. Clear. Clear.
Sorrow. Sorrow. Pain. Pain.
Hot Flashes. Sudden chills.
Stabbing pains. Slow agonies.
I drink two cups, then three bowls,
Of clear wine until I can't
Stand up against a gust of wind.
Wild geese fly over head.
They wrench my heart.
They were our friends in the old days.
Gold chrysanthemums litter
The ground, pile up, faded, dead.
This season I could not bear
To pick them. All alone,
Motionless at my window,
I watch the gathering shadows.
Fine rain sifts through the *wu t'ung* trees,
And drips, drop by drop, through the dusk.
What can I ever do now?
How can I drive off this word—
Hopelessness?

—Li Ch'ing Chao

You Above, if there be one there who knows what is going
on, repay me today for the distress I have suffered.
Inside the Earth, if there be anyone there who knows what is
going on, repay me for the distress I have suffered.
The One Who Causes Things, whoever he be, I have now
had my fill of life.
Grant me death, my sorrows are overabundant.
I do not want to live long; were I to live long, my sorrows
would be overabundant. I do not want it!

—Crow song

We wait in the darkness!
    Come, all ye who listen,
        Help in our night journey:
        Now no sun is shining;
        Now no star is glowing;
        Come show us the pathway:
        The night is not friendly;
    The moon has forgot us,
We wait in the darkness!

—Iroquois prayer

To go in the dark with a light is to know the light.
To know the dark, go dark. Go without sight,
and find that the dark, too, blooms and sings,
and is traveled by dark feet and dark wings.
                                    —Wendell Berry

Many a time I wish I were other than I am.
I weary of the solemn tide;
    of the little fields:
        of this brooding isle.

I long to be rid of the weight of duty
    and to have my part in ampler life.

O Thou, who art wisdom and pity both,
    set me free from the lordship of desire.

Help me to find my happiness
in my acceptance of what is my purpose:
    in friendly eyes;
        in quietness born of trust,
            and, most of all,
in the awareness of your presence
    in my spirit.
                                    —Alistair MacLean

Somedays the struggle just gets tired
and I want to give it a rest
I want to braid my little one's hair
and watch her jump rope
to play with her.
Somedays the rhetoric gets tiresome
no matter how true
and I want to listen to my son sing at
the drum
to sing with him.
Somedays the cause gets tedious
no matter how pressing
and I want to watch my sisters
dance
jingle dress, traditional,
to dance with them.
Somedays the struggle just gets tired
and I just want to hear the rich
laughter of my man
to enjoy his company
and to laugh with him
Somedays the struggle just gets tired.

—Renee Senolges

Weaver God, we come to you,
or more the truth—you find us,
disconnected and out of sorts.
We are disheartened by our failures,
discouraged by our weakness
        and little that we do seems worthy of your grace.
Restore our fortunes. Restore our future.
Weave for us the tapestry
    on which our lives are stretched.
Give us patience with the endless
    back and forth of shuttle, hand and effort.
We look too closely, seeing only strands and knots
and snarled threads of too-much-trying
or none-at-all.
Grant us eyes to see the whole
    of which we are a part.
In the end, we ask for gentleness with ourselves,
acceptance of our less than perfect ways.
We pray that what we do
and what you weave form patterns clear to all,
of mercy in the warp of it
and love throughout.

—Pat Kozak and Janet Schaffran

93

Captain, you know my sins.
You kept the log; you cannot have forgotten
That sleeping at the wheel. We did not founder,
And yet I closed my eyes, and a wave came
So broadside, we shivered.
Master on sea, on land, you know my weakness:
Sloth, and a love of slumber;
Days wasted, beautiful deeds
Not done when I could have done them.
Or could I? Who can say? Breathe now
The truth upon me, even if it
Blasts me.
Now is the time, the midnight hour
When I am low,
Am longing to confess.
Or wait till I grow proud again, the memory
Of all this gone from me. If it be better thus,
Smite then. You are the swordsman,
I am the receiver. As you will,
O, executioner with lifted arm.
My neck is bare.

—Mark Van Doren

In a dark time, the eye begins to see,
I meet my shadow in the deepening shade;
I hear my echo in the echoing wood—
A lord of nature weeping to a tree.
I live between the heron and the wren,
Beasts of the hill and serpents of the den.

What's madness but nobility of soul
At odds with circumstance? The day's on fire!
I know the purity of pure despair,
My shadow pinned against a sweating wall.
That place among the rocks—is it a cave,
Or winding path? The edge is what I have . . .
                              —Theodore Roethke

The Dark Night of Our Soul

When sorrow comes, let us accept it simply, as a part of life. Let the heart be open to pain; let it be stretched by it. All the evidence we have says that this is the better way. An open heart never grows bitter. Or if it does, it cannot remain so. In the desolate hour, there is an outcry; a clenching of the hands upon emptiness; a burning pain of bereavement; a weary ache of loss. But anguish, like ecstasy, is not forever. There comes a gentleness, a returning quietness, a restoring stillness. This, too, is a door to life. Here, also, is a deepening of meaning—and it can lead to dedication; a going forward to the triumph of the soul, the conquering of the wilderness. And in the process will come a deepening inward knowledge that in the final reckoning, all is well.

—A. Powell Davies

I love the dark hours of my being.
My mind deepens into them.
There I can find, as in old letters,
the days of my life, already lived,
and held like a legend, and understood.

Then the knowing comes: I can open
to another life that's wide and timeless.

So I am sometimes like a tree
rustling over a gravesite
and making real the dream
of the one its living roots
embrace:

a dream once lost
among the sorrows and songs.
            —Rainer Maria Rilke (translated by
                Anita Barrows and Joanna Macy)

This being human is a guest house.
Every morning is a new arrival.

A joy, a depression, a meanness,
some momentary awareness comes
as an unexpected visitor.

Welcome and entertain them all!
Even if they're a crowd of sorrows,
who violently sweep your house
empty of its furniture,
still, treat each guest honorably.
He may be clearing you out
for some new delight.

The dark thought, the shame, the malice,
meet them at the door laughing,
and invite them in.

Be grateful for whoever comes,
because each has been sent
as a guide from beyond.

—Rumi

PART FOUR

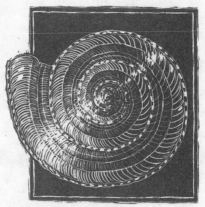

Prayers for Solidarity
and Justice

THE PRAYERS and poems in this chapter encourage us to stretch our hearts to embrace more of this world. They call us to stand beside the wounded and the defenseless, to acknowledge those who are despised or ostracized, and to open our hearts in solidarity. This is not just a political agenda—it is central to the meaning of our lives. What the world needs most is people who are less constricted by prejudice. It needs more love, more generosity, more mercy, and more openness. We are meant to be brothers and sisters, a family of nations.

> By working in this manner,
> for the sake of the land and people
> to be in vital relation
> with each other,
> we will have life,
> and it will continue.

> —Simon Ortiz

As we approach the new millennium, there is a gathering movement of people engaged in social causes. In response to several decades of increased anxiety about violence, drugs, and the fate of our children and our land, we are witnessing the resurgence of activism, of people making things happen for the good of all. From Sri Lanka to Kansas, people are joining hands to care for those in need—feeding the hungry, sheltering the homeless, establishing AIDS prevention units, restoring wild habitats. Recent statistics show that over 90 million Americans, nearly half the adult population, spend over four hours a week in volunteer activities.

What is happening here? In times of major change and social stress, people are challenged to stand up for what they believe. Perhaps this is the hidden blessing released by the suffering of the world.

The voices in this chapter of *Life Prayers* urge us to tear down the walls that separate us, to build relationships, and to work toward equality and fairness. Discovering how to pray with others we do not know, who are different from us, or who suffer in ways beyond our comprehension, is an essential and profoundly spiritual task. When I stand in solidarity with all life my experience of living changes. I am no longer a private person concerned only with taking care of me and mine. Solidarity means recognizing that the well-being of those with whom I share this planet—all people and all species—is also my own. It means that whatever situation may come before me I will try to do no harm, to relieve suffering, and to offer love. This is the compassionate heart of all religious traditions and the spiritual basis for all social action.

These prayers of solidarity and justice are our moral birthright. They offer us guidance in difficult times and solace for the grief of the world:

They sing of a life
free and simple,
with time for one another,
and for people's needs,
based on the dignity of the human person,
at one with nature's beauty . . .

—Catholic Bishops of Appalachia

O Lord,
    open my eyes that I may see the needs of others;
    open my ears that I may hear their cries;
    open my heart so that they need not be without succor;

    let me not be afraid to defend the weak because of the
    anger of the strong,
      nor afraid to defend the poor because of the
      anger of the rich.

Show me where love and hope and faith are needed,
    and use me to bring them to those places.

And so open my eyes and my ears
    that I may this coming day be able to do some work of
    peace for thee.
Amen.

—Alan Paton

104

We are the generation that stands between the fires:
behind us the flame and smoke
that rose from Auschwitz and from Hiroshima;
before us the nightmare of a Flood of Fire,
the flame and smoke that consume all Earth.
It is our task to make from fire not an all-consuming blaze
but the light in which we see each other fully.
All of us different,
all of us bearing One Spark.
We light these fires to see more clearly
that the Earth and all who live as part of it
are not for burning.
We light these fires to see more clearly
the rainbow in our many-colored faces.

Blessed is the One within the many.
Blessed are the Many who make one.

—Arthur Waskow

Mother of Exiles, Shelter of the Homeless,
we are in need of your mercy.
We ask your blessing on your children everywhere
who are in danger today.
Bless all who suffer from injustice.
Shelter them in the warmth of your love
and safeguard them from the evil that rages around them.
Turn our eyes and hearts to their needs
and give us courage to act for their good.
We ask this, relying on your compassion
and confident of your love. Amen.

—Pat Kozak

There will be a morning song
for those who clean the dust
from the children's bruises
the blood of the wounds from bullets
those who wipe the sleep
from the eyes of the weary
and whose labour shields
the frail bodies of the old
those whose pain is multiplied
by the pleas of their young
scarred by the precision
of their inquisitors
who refuse to retreat in battle
and who are dying with the sum of this knowledge
There will be a future.

—Iyamide Hazeley

O God, our Father and Mother,
we confess today that your own sons and daughters in Christ
have let you down.
Dominated by our fears,
we have trampled and smothered one another.
We have smothered the tenderness of man;
we have smothered the creative thinking of women.
Help women to discover honest and life-giving relationships;
help men to open their hearts to each other in friendship;
help us to create a community of brothers and sisters,
where we can live with each
other in creative community
    man with man
    woman with woman
    man with woman. Amen.

               —Kerstin Lindqvist and Ulla Bardh

What actions are
most excellent?

To gladden the heart
of a human being.
To feed the hungry.
To help the afflicted.
To lighten the sorrow
of the sorrowful.
To remove the wrongs
of the injured.
That person is the
most beloved of God
who does most good
to God's creatures.
                    —The Prophet Muhammed

Blessed are the poor in spirit:
    for theirs is the kingdom of heaven.
Blessed are they that mourn: for they shall be comforted.
Blessed are the meek: for they shall inherit the earth.
Blessed are they who hunger and thirst after righteousness:
    for they shall be filled.
Blessed are the merciful: for they shall obtain mercy.
Blessed are the pure in heart: for they shall see God.
Blessed are the peacemakers: for they shall be called the
    children of God.

                                      —Matthew 5:3–9

May our eyes remain open even in the face of tragedy.
May we not become disheartened.
May we find in the dissolution
  of our apathy and denial,
  the cup of the broken heart.
May we discover the gift of the fire burning
  in the inner chamber of our being—
  burning great and bright enough
  to transform any poison.
May we offer the power of our sorrow to the service
  of something greater than ourselves.
May our guilt not rise up to form
  yet another defensive wall.
May the suffering purify and not paralyze us.
May we endure; may sorrow bond us and not separate us.
May we realize the greatness of our sorrow
  and not run from its touch or its flame.
May clarity be our ally and wisdom our support.
May our wrath be cleansing, cutting through
  the confusion of denial and greed.
May we not be afraid to see or speak our truth.
May the bleakness of the wasteland be dispelled.
May the soul's journey be revealed
  and the true hunger fed.
May we be forgiven for what we have forgotten
  and blessed with the remembrance
  of who we really are.

—The Terma Collective

Great Spirit, give us hearts to understand;
never to take from creation's beauty more than we give;
never to destroy wantonly for the furtherance of greed;
never to deny to give our hands
for the building of Earth's beauty;
never to take from her what we cannot use.
Give us hearts to understand
that to destroy Earth's music is to create confusion;
that to wreck her appearance is to blind us to beauty;
that to callously pollute her fragrance
is to make a house of stench;
that as we care for her she will care for us. Amen.
—U.N. Environmental Sabbath

In our mindlessness, we are
    corrupting the Earth,
    poisoning the air,
    disrupting the fire,
    polluting the water.
We are making life impossible
    for our fellow creatures
    and for ourselves.
We are destroying the heart of the universe.

Come Holy Spirit of Earth,
    air, fire, and water.
Enkindle in us the fire of your love.
Send your spirit over the waters
    and we shall be created.
And we shall renew the face of the Earth.

                                        —Daniel Martin

The earth belongs to the Lord,
   and everything on it is his.
For he founded it in empty space
   and breathed his own life-breath into it,
filling it with manifold creatures,
   each one precious in his sight.

Who is fit to hold power
   and worthy to act in God's place?
Those with a passion for the truth,
   who are horrified by injustice,
who act with mercy to the poor
   and take up the cause of the helpless,
who have let go of selfish concerns
   and see the whole earth as sacred,
refusing to exploit her creatures
   or to foul her waters and lands.
Their strength is in their compassion;
   God's light shines through their hearts.
Their children's children will bless them,
   and the work of their hands will endure.

   —Psalm 24 (version by Stephen Mitchell)

Giver of life and all good gifts:
Grant us also wisdom to use only what we need;
Courage to trust your bounty;
Imagination to preserve our resources;
Determination to deny frivolous excess;
And inspiration to sustain through temptation
                                        —Patricia Winters

With resources scarcer and scarcer
    I vow with all beings
to consider the law of proportion:
my have is another's have-not.
                                        —Robert Aitken

Incline us O God!
to think humbly of ourselves,
to be saved only in the examination of our own conduct,
to consider our fellow-creatures with kindness,
and to judge of all they say and do with the charity
which we would desire from them ourselves.

—Jane Austen

Make us worthy, Lord,
to serve others throughout the world
who live and die
in poverty or hunger,
Give them, through our hands, this day their daily bread,
and by our understanding love,
give peace and joy.

—Mother Teresa

But we have only begun
to love the earth.

We have only begun
to imagine the fulness of life.

How could we tire of hope?
—so much is in the bud.

How can desire fail?
—we have only begun

to imagine justice and mercy,
only begun to envision

how it might be
to live as siblings with beast
    and flower,
not as oppressors.

Surely our river
cannot already be hastening
into the sea of nonbeing?

Surely it cannot
drag, in the silt,
all that is innocent?

Not yet, not yet—
there is too much broken
that must be mended,

too much hurt we have done
    to each other
that cannot yet be forgiven.

We have only begun to know
the power that is in us if we
    would join
our solitudes in the
    communion of struggle.

So much is unfolding that must
complete its gesture,

so much is in bud.
            —Denise Levertov

Where there are ruptures in creation,
   we are aroused to peace,
Where there is disquietude
   we are invited to balance.
Where there is discord
   we are attuned to resonance.
In and through the pain of our
     planet
   we are called to make our Easter with
   the Earth
From collapse and devastation
   we discover within the risen heart of the
     universe
     cosmic peace,
     profound harmony,
     deep balance,
     compassionate resonance,
     pentecost for the planet and
     geo-justice with the Earth.
                —James Conlon

We who have lost our sense and our senses—
Our touch, our smell, our vision of who we are;
we who frantically force and press all things,
without rest for body or spirit,
hurting our Earth and injuring ourselves; We call a halt.

We want to rest.
We need to rest and allow the Earth to rest.
We need to reflect and to rediscover the mystery that lives in us,
that is the ground of every unique expression of life,
the source of the fascination that calls all things to communion.
We declare an Earth Holy Day, a space of quiet:
for simple being and letting be;
for recovering the great forgotten truths.

—Daniel Martin

May God bless us not with clean air alone,
But the will to keep our air clean.

May God bless us not with a vision of a healthy planet alone,
But with the will to do all in our power to restore and maintain
    our planet's health.

May God bless us not with a change of heart in the great world
    leaders alone to save our planet,
But with a change in our own heart to use our own power to save
    the planet.

May the blessing of God not bring to us saints alone,
But make of us saints greater than any we imagine.

—Daniel J. McGill

As no one desires the slightest suffering
nor ever has enough of happiness,
there is no difference between myself and others,
so let me make others joyfully happy.

May those feeble with cold find warmth,
and may those oppressed with heat be cooled
by the boundless waters that pour forth
from the great clouds of the Bodhisattvas.

May the rains of lava, blazing stones and weapons
from now on become a rain of flowers,
and may all battling with weapons
from now on be a playful exchange of flowers.

May the naked find clothing,
the hungry find food;
may the thirsty find water
and delicious drinks.

May the frightened cease to be afraid
and those bound be freed;
may the powerless find power,
and may people think of benefiting one another.

For as long as space endures
and for as long as living beings remain,
until then may I too abide
to dispel the misery of the world.

—Shantideva

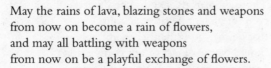

Please pacify the uninterrupted miseries
and unbearable fears,
such as famines and sicknesses,
that torment powerless beings
completely oppressed by inexhaustible
and violent evils,
and henceforth lead us from suffering states
and place us in an ocean of happiness and joy.

Those who, maddened by the demons of delusion,
commit violent negative actions
that destroy both themselves and others,
should be the object of our compassion.
May the hosts of undisciplined beings
fully gain the eye that knows
what to abandon and practice,
and be granted a wealth
of loving kindness and friendliness.

Through the force of dependent-arising,
which by nature is profound
and empty of appearances,
the force of the Words of Truth,
the power of the kindness of the Three Jewels
and the true power of non-deceptive actions
and their effects;
may my prayer of truth
be accomplished quickly and without hindrance.

> —His Holiness the Fourteenth Dalai Lama

Thousands of years
of history have passed . . .
and during all that time
human beings
have fought, killed,
plundered and wronged each other
in every possible way.
Of such stuff history is made.

But also during that time,
other human beings
have quietly and patiently persevered
in the development
of the arts, crafts,
inventions, ideas and programs.
From these millions of creative persons,
most of them unnoticed and unknown
in the upheavals of history,
have come the good and lasting things
in the sum of human culture.
—Barbara G. Walker

I would like you to know
That we were not all like that.
That some of us spent our lives
Working for Peace
Speaking for animals
Tending the Earth.
And that when you find
The mass graves
And the abattoirs
And the laboratories
Please understand
That we were not all like that.

—Mary de La Valette

In spite of everything, I still believe
that people are really good at heart.
I simply can't build up my hopes on a foundation
consisting of confusion, misery, and death.
I see the world gradually being turned into a wilderness,
I hear the ever-approaching thunder, which will destroy us, too,
I can feel the suffering of millions, and yet,
if I look up into the heavens,
I think that it will all come right,
that this cruelty will end,
and that peace and tranquility will return again.
In the meantime, I must uphold my ideals,
for perhaps the time will come
when I shall be able to carry them out.

—Anne Frank

Dear Great Spirit who is known by many names,

Do you hear the prayers of people in prison, of refugees walking on roads because a war has forced them from their homes, of people knowing that war and genocide is in their place and their time may come any time? Do you hear my prayer every day as I open the newspaper that friends in these vulnerable situations be spared? If you hear those prayers, how is it that these horrors continue every day?

I don't mean to challenge the way things are going, but the growing darkness sometimes obliterates my view of the glorious natural world everywhere and the miracles of life to be cherished all around.

My heart is grateful for the many saints found in these terrible situations. Bless them and give them endurance. May they feel sustained by the warmth of the sun on their bodies. And, oh mighty spirit, if I can help carry any part of the load for these people, if in any way I can help, give me the wisdom to pour myself into the task with ease and grace. If I can be a companion for the prisoner, carry the refugee on the road or scream about genocide so that someone wakes up from a sleep and stops the killing, let me do it. May I find the courage not to hide from the harsh truth of what is happening in my world in my time. Let me attend to every blossoming life around me with appreciation and love. Show me the light in the darkness.

—Fran Peavey

The time for healing of the wounds has come.
The time to build is upon us . . .
We pledge ourselves to liberate all our people
from the continuing bondage of poverty, deprivation,
suffering, gender and other discrimination . . .
There is no easy road to freedom . . .
None of us acting alone can achieve success.
We must therefore act together as a united people,
for reconciliation, for nation building,
for the birth of a new world.

—Nelson Mandela

The threat to our salvation is the clash of peoples:
Jews and Arabs,
offspring of a single father,
separated in youth by jealousy,
in adolescence by fear,
in adulthood by power,
in old age by habit.
It is time to break these habits of hate
and create new habits:
habits of the heart
that will awake within us
the causeless love of redemption and peace.
—Rabbi Rami M. Shapiro

Lead us from death to life,
from falsehood to truth.
Lead us from despair to hope,
from fear to trust.
Let peace fill our hearts,
our world, our universe.
Let us dream together,
pray together,
work together,
to build one world
of peace and justice for all.
—Anonymous

I breathe in rain
I breathe out green
I breathe in wind
I breathe out sky
I breathe in laughter
I breathe out happiness
I breathe in her
I breathe out poetry
I breathe in daughters and sons
I breathe out hope
I breathe in words
I breathe out mountains
I breathe in sage
I breathe out clarity
I breathe in dust
I breathe out the bones
   of my people
I breathe in oppression
I breathe out liberation
I breathe in fire
I breathe out clouds
I breathe in ink
I breathe out veins
I breathe in Buddha
I breathe out Mexican.

—Arnoldo García

Unfolded out of the folds of the woman man comes
unfolded, and is always to come unfolded,
Unfolded only out of the superbest woman of the earth
is to come the superbest man of the earth,
Unfolded out of the friendliest woman is to come the
friendliest man,
Unfolded only out of the perfect body of a woman can
a man be form'd of perfect body,
Unfolded only out of the inimitable poems of woman
can come the poems of man, (only thence have my
poems come;)
Unfolded out of the strong and arrogant woman I love,
only thence can appear the strong and arrogant man
I love,
Unfolded by brawny embraces from the well-muscled
woman I love, only thence come the brawny
embraces of the man,
Unfolded out of the folds of the woman's brain come
all the folds of the man's brain, duly obedient,
Unfolded out of the justice of the woman all justice is
unfolded,
Unfolded out of the sympathy of the woman is all
sympathy;
A man is a great thing upon the earth and through
eternity, but every jot of greatness of man is
unfolded out of woman;
First the man is shaped in the woman, he can then be
shaped in himself.

—Walt Whitman

If copper were the color of your skin
    instead of pale
    light tan
    or white
would you identify with those people of the sun,
the warriors, the strong
    the forgiving . . . ?

would you remember the loss
the disappearances of people
    and culture surrounded by guns &
lives decimated?

If copper were the color of your skin
would you understand my needs
    and my anger?

would you understand my loss
and join with me in struggle
    returning the gift
    to our people?

                    —Sarah Lyons

Today
we will not be invisible nor silent
as the pilgrims of yesterday
continue their war of attrition
forever trying, but never succeeding
    in their battle to rid the americas of us
convincing others and ourselves
    that we have been assimilated and eliminated
        but we remember who we are
        we are the spirit of endurance that lives
in the cities and reservations of north america
and in the barrios and countryside of Nicaragua, Chile
Guatemala, El Salvador
    and in all the earth and rivers of the americas
                              —Victoria Lena Manyarrows

To the nations of the Native American Indians,
    as a citizen of the United States I say, please
    forgive me and please forgive us.
On behalf of my ancestors and the group conscience
    of all America, I deeply apologize for
    the wrongs, so cruel, that have been inflicted
    upon your people.
So many lives lost, yet still they haunt the
    psyche of all people of goodwill,

We ask that the spirit of God give us absolution.
We as a nation have wronged.
Now we as a nation make amends.
How sorry we are for the suffering of your
  people.
If we could rewrite history, we would.
We cannot, but God can.
May history begin again.
May the spirit of your people now be reborn.

For we embrace and honor the spirit of the
  Native American tribes.
We bless and commit to the good of your
  children and your children's children.
May we begin anew.
May your star rise high in the sky of this nation
  and all others.
May the wrongs of the past now be made right
  that your nation might be blessed, that our
  nation might be blessed.
So be it.
Please, God, make these things right in love,
  in healing, in mercy, in grace.
Amen.

—Marianne Williamson

We speak of the people
who live in this land,
people who love nature's freedom
and beauty,
who are alive with song
and poetry.

But many of these people are also poor
and suffer oppression.
The poor of our land
have been wounded,
but they are not crushed.
The Spirit still lives.

Their struggles and their poetry
together keep alive
    a dream
    a tradition
    a longing
    a promise
which is not just their dream,
but the voiceless vision
buried beneath life's bitterness
wherever it is found.

They sing of a life
free and simple,
with time for one another,
and for people's needs,
based on the dignity of the human person,
at one with nature's beauty,
crowned by poetry.
If that dream dies,
all our struggles
die with it.
This struggle of resistance
is a struggle against violence—
against institutional violence
which sometimes subtly,
sometimes brutally,
attacks human dignity and life.
At stake is the spirit
of all our humanity.

—Pastoral Letter,
Catholic Bishops of Appalachia

Prayers for Solidarity and Justice

I have a dream today.
I have a dream that one day every valley shall be exalted,
   every hill and mountain shall be made low,
   and the crooked places will be made straight,
   and the glory of the Lord shall be revealed,
   and all flesh shall see it together.
This is our hope. This is the faith with which I return.
With this faith we will be able to hew out of the mountain of despair
   a stone of hope.
With this faith we will be able to transform the jangling discords
   of our nation
   into a beautiful symphony of brotherhood.
With this faith we will be able to work together, to pray together,
   to struggle together, to go to jail together, to stand up
   for freedom together, knowing that we will be free one day.
This will be the day when all of God's children will be able to sing
   with a new meaning

   My country, 'tis of thee
   Sweet land of liberty,
   Of thee I sing:
   Land where my fathers died,
   Land of the pilgrim's pride,
   From every mountain-side
   Let freedom ring.

And if America is to be a great nation this must become true.
So let freedom ring from the prodigious hilltops of New Hampshire.
Let freedom ring from the mighty mountains of New York.
Let freedom ring from the heightening Alleghenies of Pennsylvania!
Let freedom ring from the snowcapped Rockies of Colorado!
Let freedom ring from the curvaceous peaks of California!
But not only that; let freedom ring from Stone Mountain of Georgia!

Let freedom ring from Lookout Mountain of Tennessee!
Let freedom ring from every hill and molehill of Mississippi.
From every mountainside, let freedom ring.
When we let freedom ring, when we let it ring
from every village and every hamlet, from every state and every city,
we will be able to speed up the day when all of God's children,
black men and white men, Jews and Gentiles, Protestants and Catholics,
will be able to join hands and sing in the words of the old Negro spiritual,
"Free at last! thank God almighty, we are free at last!"
—Martin Luther King, Jr.

138

May the atmosphere we breathe
breathe fearlessness into us:
fearlessness on earth
and fearlessness in heaven!
May fearlessness guard us
behind and before!
May fearlessness surround us
above and below!
May we be without fear
of friend and foe!
May we be without fear
by night and by day!
Let all the world be my friend!
—Atharva Veda XIX, 15

The USA slowly lost her mandate
in the middle and later twentieth century
it never gave the mountains and rivers,
    trees and animals,
        a vote.

all the people turned away from it
    myths die; even continents are impermanent

    Turtle Island returned.
    my friend broke open a dried coyote-scat

---

removed a ground squirrel tooth
pierced it, hung it
from the gold ring
in his ear.

We look to the future with pleasure
we need no fossil fuel
get power within
grow strong on less.

Grasp the tools and move in rhythm side by side
   flash gleams of wit and silent knowledge
      eye to eye
sit still like cats or snakes or stones
   as whole and holding as
      the blue black sky.
gentle and innocent as wolves
     as tricky as a prince.

At work in our place:

in the service
of the wilderness
of life
of death
of the Mother's breasts!

—Gary Snyder

The land. The people.
They are in relation to each other.
We are in a family with each other.
The land has worked with us.
And the people have worked with it.

This is true:
Working for the land
and the people—it means life
and its continuity.
Working not just for the people,
but for the land too.
We are not alone in our life;
we cannot expect to be.
The land has given us our life,
and we must give life back to it.

The land has worked for us
to give us life—
breathe and drink and eat from it
gratefully—
and we must work for it
to give it life.
Within this relation of family,
it is possible to generate life.

This is the work involved.
Work is creative then.
It is what makes for reliance,
relying upon the relation of land and people.
The people and the land are reliant
upon each other.
This is the kind of self-reliance
that has been—
before the liars, thieves and killers—
and this is what we must continue
to work for.

By working in this manner,
for the sake of the land and people
to be in vital relation
with each other,
we will have life,
and it will continue.

We have been told many things,
but we know this to be true:
the land and the people.

—Simon Ortiz

Alone, you can fight,
you can refuse, you can
take what revenge you can
but they roll over you.

But two people fighting
back to back can cut through
a mob, a snake-dancing file
can break a cordon, an army
can meet an army.

Two people can keep each other
sane, can give support, conviction,
love, massage, hope, sex.
Three people are a delegation,
a committee, a wedge. With four
you can play bridge and start
an organization. With six
you can rent a whole house,
eat pie for dinner with no
seconds, and hold a fund raising party.

A dozen make a demonstration.
A hundred fill a hall.
    A thousand have solidarity and your own newsletter;
ten thousand, power and your own paper;
a hundred thousand, your own media;
ten million, your own country.

It goes on one at a time,
it starts when you care
to act, it starts when you do
it again after they said no,
it starts when you say We
and know who you mean, and each
day you mean one more.

—Marge Piercy

PART FIVE

Womansprayer

Today women throughout the world are reawakening to the feminine face of the Divine. After a five-thousand-year reign of masculine values and male icons in the religions of the Western world, we are privileged to witness a global reappearance of the sacred identity of the feminine in the arts and in religious ceremony. Women's history is revealing a legacy of female leadership, authority, and wisdom dating back some thirty thousand years. It is inspiring a new spiritual vision among the women of this century and broadening the prospects for our daughters and sons.

While this expanded approach to comprehending the sacred is not made up exclusively of women, it is natural that women are leading the way. For it is in large measure the spiritual meaning of women's life experience that has been undervalued, and it is women's stories that are today providing greater opportunities for this kind of revelation. Women of courage and men of conscience are called upon through this tradition of *womansprayer* to reintegrate the wisdom of the life-affirming feminine.

> ten thousand years I have been sleeping
>   and now I am being wakened.
> my heavy eyelashes are the woods;
> They are beckoning

My heart the clouds are surprised
　　because they are calling me, calling me. . . .
　　　　　　　　　　　　　　　　　　—Masika Szilagyi

　　　　The voices of individual women in this chapter tell us of the sacred as it enters into everyday life. We are shown the strength required to survive, the power implicit in vulnerability, the necessity of the descent into the dark, and the ability of our bodies to receive and give Divine energy.

　　　　As we "listen to the Madres, and the Women in Black, and the African mamas" and white sisters share their stories, we find ourselves reborn along with them into a deeply embodied spirituality. Once again the cycles of a woman's body, her menstruation, birthing, and mothering experiences are celebrated and honored. Her sexuality and intuition are considered holy, and she is recognized as a sacred daughter of Gaia, the ground of all being.

Here is your sacrament
　　Take. Eat. this is my body
　　this real milk, thin, sweet, bluish,
　　which I give for the life of the world. . . .

Here is your bread of life.
Here is the blood by which you live in me.
　　　　　　　　　　　　　　　　　　—Robin Morgan

　　　　Implicit in these prayers is a revaluing of woman's experience. These women accept full spiritual responsibility for their lives. They

---

ask for and give forgiveness. They seek to fathom rather than flatter themselves. They let their hearts lead the way. As a consequence we come to know and honor more deeply the unique qualities of a woman's inner reality.

The challenge of these voices is clear. Women are demanding that their experience be taken seriously. They are reminding us that their agenda for freedom, equality, and personal security has not yet been satisfied. They are inviting us to participate with them in realizing a greater wholeness within ourselves, our communities, and our world.

Ten thousand years I have been sleeping
   and now I am being wakened.
My heavy eyelashes are the woods;
They are beckoning.
My heart, the clouds are surprised
   because they are calling me, calling me.
My earth body is bedecked
   with a thousand flowers,
Many breasts of mine,
   the mountains joyfully rearing their tips,
They are calling! They are calling!
I want to embrace all the sad and the lost.
All wrongs my hands shall doom to death.
I am the defender of every woman
As I am the defender of my holy self.
Earthmother I am, the Only One;
Everything sprang from me;
I carry the seed of all creation;
I am the bestower of life alone.
Oh, oh, oh, I am awake!
Oh, I am answering the call . . .

                    —Masika Szilagyi

She Who has power to open the womb
has done great things for me.

Holy is Her name.

Her mercy flows
through mother to daughter

from generation to generation.

Her maternal strength
strikes at the roots of evil,
and it departs.

She pushes the proud
from the pinnacles of power
and lifts up little people.

She feeds her hungry daughters,

but those who are filled to the brim
with opportunity,
She sends away.

She soothes all those who turn to Her,
remembering Her compassion,

keeping Her promise to
Her progeny forever.

—Miriam Therese Winter

Bright lady of the waters, untamable woman flowing with
   the strength and beauty of the women's revolution!
You break the chains of our oppression with your force,
   while lapping inside us a love and sexuality.
We drink of your life force and ask you to bless the eternal
   solidarity and love between all women; we flow from
   the same womanspirit.
May we join together and celebrate this!

—Zsuzsanna E. Budapest

Strength comes from seeing:
the eye that fiercely holds the mark
so arrow surely follows.
Do not be deterred!
And when you have the need,
I offer my protection—
Only call
and I am there.

O my sisters, come!
There is pleasure in leafy glen,
in sinew to race with the wind!

O come!
We gather now on sacred ground,
and bonding, link the earth around,
to free the spirit, heal the wound—
a sisterhood of wind and moon.

     —Nancy Rose Meeker

Women, please let your own sun, your
concentrated energy, your own submerged
authentic vital power shine out from you.

We are no longer the moon.
Today we are truly the sun.
We will build shining golden cathedrals
at the top of crystal mountains, East of
the Land of the Rising Sun.

Women, when you paint your own portrait,
do not forget to put the golden dome at
the top of your head.

—Raicho Hiratsuko

Blessed be my brain
    that I may conceive of my own power.
Blessed be my breast
    that I may give sustenance to those I love.
Blessed be my womb
    that I may create what I choose to create.
Blessed be my knees
    that I may bend so as not to break.
Blessed be my feet
    that I may walk in the path of my highest will.

—Robin Morgan

Praise and love to those who seek,
to those who know and those who speak,
to those who smile with tender eyes,
whose wisdom penetrates the lies,
to those who sing and those who cry.
For those who fight for right and die.
To those who live to ripe old age,
to great grandmother, the family sage.
Praise and love to my daughters.
To those unborn and yet to come,
we lead you on with song and hum.
From other worlds and through birth-waters,
come forth Child, beloved daughter.
Praise and love to the Mothers of the World.
Praise and love to the Sisters of the World.
Praise and love to the Women of the World.
Praise and love to my daughters.

—Luisah Teish

155

I listen to the women of Rio
when they try to speak
of street children murdered,
and my heart is breaking.

I listen to the women of Chernobyl
tell of childish blank faces
grown old and lifeless
and my heart is breaking.

I listen to the women of Bhopal
whisper the grotesqueness
of deformity and disease,
and my heart is breaking . . .

I listen to the women of Addis Ababa
describing empty stomachs
and drought,
and my heart is breaking.

I listen to the women of Cyprus
and Ireland and Sri Lanka
and South Africa.
I hear conflict's pain,
and my heart is breaking.

But also,
I listen to the Madres, and the Women in Black,
and the African mamas. I listen to
the young women of Asia and the Pacific Rim.
I listen to the female voices of North Africa,
and the Middle East and Eastern Europe.
And I hear
the Power of Everywoman,
Everywhere.
Then, I rejoice,
I hope,
I take heart.

—Elayne Clift

We are Women-Church.
We claim our power.
We proclaim our economic power.
We are breadmakers and breadwinners.
We affirm our responsibility
to share the earth's goods with the earth's people,
to build structures of economic justice for all.

We proclaim our spiritual power.
We are healers and holy, priests and prophets.
We affirm our responsibility to break bread
and lift a cup in the name of liberation.

We proclaim our sexual power.
We are moral agents who make decisions
about our bodies.
We affirm our responsibility to make choices
that promote dignity and reflect love.

We proclaim our political power.
We are voters and change agents.
We affirm our responsibility
to influence public policy and to build a new world,
starting with the struggling poor.

—Mary E. Hunt

We are female human beings poised on the edge of the new millennium. We are the majority of our species, yet we have dwelt in the shadows. We are the invisible, the illiterate, the laborers, the refugees, the poor.

And we vow: No more.

We are the women who hunger—for rice, home, freedom, each other, ourselves.

We are the women who thirst—for clean water and laughter, literacy and love. We have existed at all times, in every society. We have survived femicide. We have rebelled—and left clues.

We are continuity, weaving future from past, logic with lyric.

We are the women who stand in our sense, and shout Yes.

We are the women who wear broken bones, voices, minds, hearts—but we are the women who dare whisper No.

We are the women whose souls no fundamentalist cage can contain.

We are the women who refuse to permit the sowing of death in our gardens, air, rivers, seas.

We are the women men warned us about.

We are each precious, unique, necessary. We are strengthened and blessed and relieved at not having to be all the same. We are the daughters of longing. We are the mothers in labor to birth the politics of the 21st Century.

—Robin Morgan and friends

Womansprayer

theres more poor than nonpoor
theres more colored than noncolored
theres more women than men

all over the world the poor woman of color is the mainstay of
the little daddy centred family which is the bottom-line of
big daddys industrial civilization

when she gets off her knees and stands up straight the whole
thing can/will collapse

have you noticed that even now she is flexing her shoulder
muscles and strengthening her thigh and leg muscles?

and her spine is learning to stretch out long her brain and heart
are pumping new energy already you can see the load crack-
ing at the center as she pushes it off her

she is holding up the whole world
what you gonna do?
you cant stop her
you gonna just stand there and watch her with your mouth open?
or are you gonna try to get down?
you cant stop her
she is holding up the whole world

—Hattie Gossett

I
am a black woman
tall as a cypress
strong
beyond all definition still
defying place
and time
and circumstance
   assailed
      impervious
         indestructible
Look
  on me and be
renewed

                —Mari Evans

161

Yo soy mujer
I am woman. . . .
I am not one.
I am not two.
I am the many
the multitude,
the full force
of women throughout
history throughout
the world.
And we are angry.
And we are powerful.
And we are
truth-tellers
And we are
passionately tender:
And we are claiming
justice, now!
. . . Somos la vida, la
fuerza, la mujer
. . . We are life, strength,
woman
en marcha de justicia
empezamos a florecer
on the march for justice
we begin to blossom.
                    —Maria Elena del Valle

Ain't I a woman?
    Look at me
Look at my arm!
    I have plowed and planted
and gathered into barns
    and no man could head me. . . .
And ain't I a woman?
    I could work as much
And eat as much as a man—
    When I could get it—
And bear the lash as well
    and ain't I a woman?
I have born thirteen children
    and seen most all sold into slavery
and when I cried out a mother's grief
    none but Jesus hear me . . .
and ain't I a woman? . . .
    If the first woman God ever made
was strong enough to turn the world
    upside down, all alone
together women ought to be able to turn it
    rightside up again.

                                —Sojourner Truth

163

This is a poem for a woman doing dishes.
This is a poem for a woman doing dishes.
It must be repeated.
It must be repeated,
again and again,
again and again,
because the woman doing dishes
because the woman doing dishes
has trouble hearing
has trouble hearing.

And this is another poem for a woman
cleaning the floor
who cannot hear at all.
Let us have a moment of silence
for the woman who cleans the floor.

And here is one more poem
for the woman at home
with children.
You never see her at night.
Stare at an empty space and imagine her there,
the woman with children
because she cannot be here to speak
for herself
and listen
to what you think
she might say.

—Susan Griffin

At last free,
at last I am a woman free!
No more tied to the kitchen,
stained amid the stained pots,
no more bound to the husband
who thought me less
than the shade he wove with his hands.
No more anger, no more hunger,
I sit now in the shade of my own tree.
Meditating thus, I am happy, I am serene.

        —Sumangalamata

Here lies a poor woman who was always tired,
For she lived in a place where help wasn't hired.
Her last words on earth were, Dear friends I am going
Where washing ain't done nor sweeping nor sewing,
And everything there is exact to my wishes,
For there they don't eat and there's no washing of
  dishes.
Don't mourn for me now, don't mourn for me never,
For I'm going to do nothing for ever and ever.

        —Anonymous

166

We ask forgiveness
of one another,
woman to woman,
sister to sister.

We ask forgiveness
of one another,
as children of God,
as friend to friend.

Too many times
have we failed to stand
together
in solidarity.
Too many times
have we judged one another,
condemning those things
we did not understand.

We ask forgiveness
for assuming we know
all there is to know
about each other,
for presuming to speak
for each other,
for defining,
confining,
claiming,
naming,
limiting,
labeling,
conditioning,
interpreting,
and consequently oppressing
each other.
　　　　—Medical Mission
　　　　　　　　Sisters

I seek mercy
for the women stoned
and their accomplice—the darkness of the night,
for the scent of clover and the branches
on which they fell intoxicated
like quails and woodcocks,
for their scorned lives,
for their love torments,
unrelieved by compassion.
I seek mercy
for the moonlight and for the rubies,
of their skin,
for the moonlight's dusk,
for the showers of their undone hair,
for the handful of silvery branches,
for their loves naked
and damned—
for all Mary Magdalenes.

—Desanka Maksimovic

some rhythms must remain unbroken

like a dancer in an
arabesque
some women cannot carry
a child
in their arms

some come to salvation
drawn by the hands of small children

some can only make their leaps

alone.

—Mary Mackey

Before Jesus
was his mother.

Before supper
in the upper room,
breakfast in the barn.

Before the Passover Feast,
a feeding trough.
And here, the altar
of Earth, fair linens
of hay and seed.

Before his cry,
her cry.
Before his sweat
of blood,
her bleeding
and tears.
Before his offering,
hers.

Before the breaking
of bread and death,
the breaking of her
body in birth.

Before the offering
of the cup,
the offering of her
breast.
Before his blood,
her blood.
And by her body and blood
alone, his body and blood
and whole human being.

The wise ones knelt
to hear the woman's word
in wonder.
Holding up her sacred child,
her God in the form of a babe,
she said: "Receive and let
your hearts be healed
and your lives be filled
with love, for
This is my body,
This is my blood."
     —Alla Renée Bozarth

169

As it was in the beginning,
    I say:
    Here is your sacrament—

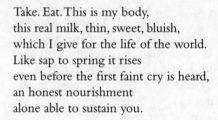

        Take. Eat. This is my body,
        this real milk, thin, sweet, bluish,
        which I give for the life of the world.
        Like sap to spring it rises
        even before the first faint cry is heard,
        an honest nourishment
        alone able to sustain you.

    I say:
    Here is your eternal testament—

        This cup, this chalice, this primordial cauldron
        of real menstrual blood
        the color of clay warm with promise,
        rhythmic, cyclical, fit for lining the uterus
        and shed for many,
        for the remission of living.

Here is your bread of life.
Here is the blood by which you live in me.
                    —Robin Morgan

I have wanted excellence in the knife-throw,
I have wanted to use my exceptionally strong and accurate arms
and my straight posture and quick electric muscles
to achieve something at the center of a crowd,
the blade piercing the bark deep,
the haft slowly and heavily vibrating like the cock.

I have wanted some epic use for my excellent body,
some heroism, some American achievement
beyond the ordinary for my extraordinary self,
magnetic and tensile, I have stood by the sandlot
and watched the boys play.

I have wanted courage, I have thought about fire
and the crossing of waterfalls, I have dragged around

my belly big with cowardice and safety,
my stool black with iron pills,
my huge breasts oozing mucus,
my legs swelling, my hands swelling,
my face swelling and darkening, my hair
falling out, my inner sex
stabbed again and again with terrible pain like a knife.
I have laid down.

I have laid down and sweated and shaken
and passed blood and feces and water and
slowly alone in the center of a circle I have
passed the new person out

Womansprayer

and they have lifted the new person free of the act
and wiped the new person free of that
language of blood like praise all over the body.

I have done what I wanted to do, Walt Whitman,
Allen Ginsberg, I have done this thing,
I and the other women this exceptional
act with the exceptional heroic body,
this giving birth, this glistening verb,
and I am putting my proud American boast
right here with the others.

—Sharon Olds

---

we need a god who bleeds now
a god whose wounds are not
some small male vengeance
some pitiful concession to
    humility
a desert swept with dryin
    marrow in honor of the
    lord

we need a god who bleeds
spreads her lunar vulva &
    showers us in shades
    of scarlet

---

thick & warm
   like the breath of her
our mothers tearing
   to let us in
this place breaks open
like our mothers bleeding

the planet is heaving
   mourning our ignorance
the moon tugs the seas
to hold her / to hold her
embrace swelling hills / i am
not wounded i am bleeding
   to life

we need a god who bleeds now
whose wounds are not
   the end of anything
                    —Ntozake Shange

For I am the first, and the last,
I am the honored one, and the scorned.
I am the whore and the holy one.
I am the wife and the virgin.
I am the mother, the daughter,
and every part of both.
I am the barren one who has borne many sons.
I am she whose wedding is great
and I have no accepted husband.
I am the midwife and the childless one,
the easing of my own labor.
I am the bride and the bridegroom
and my husband is my father.
I am the mother of my father,
the sister of my husband;
my husband is my child.

My offspring are my own birth,
the source of my power,
what happens to me is their wish.

—Thunder Perfect Mind

The first day
 I came to in the dark cold trembling
 while I gathered twigs lit them he came out
 of the cave shivered held his hands over
 the fire and said: let there be light
The second day
 I woke at dawn carried water from the river
 to wet the clay ground so the dust wouldn't
 whip his face he came out I poured water into
 his palms he washed his face looked up and
 said: Let's call the sky roof the dryness earth
 and the gathered waters the seas
The third day
 I got up early picked blue red yellow fruit
 piling small seeds between two stones ground
 kneaded roast them he awoke stretched ate the
 bread the sweet fruit said: Let the earth
 bear tender grasses grasses with seeds fruit
 trees.
The fourth day
 I awoke suddenly swept the yard with a branch
 of leaves soaked the laundry scrubbed the
 pots cleaned the tools he woke as I sharpened
 the scythe rolled over and said: Let heavenly
 bodies light the sky to divide day from night.

The fifth day
> I rode in the morning filled the troughs
> gave the horses hay milked the cows
> sheared the sheep grazed the goats stuffed
> the geese cut nettles for the ducklings
> ground corn for the hens cooked slops for
> the pigs threw the dog a bone poured the cat
> its milk he yawned slowly rubbed the sleep from his
> eyes and said: Let everything multiply and
> grow and cover the earth

The sixth day
> Pains woke me I gave birth to my child cleaned
> swaddled nursed him he leaved over let the
> little hand squeeze his thumb he smiled at
> his likeness and saw that truly all of his creation
> was good

The seventh day
> The baby's crying woke me I quickly changed
> his diapers nursed him he quieted down I
> lit the fire aired the apartment brought
> up the newspaper watered the plants dusted quietly
> made breakfast the smell of coffee woke him he turned
> on the radio lit a cigarette and blessed the seventh day

—Eva Toth

PART SIX

Initiations

OUR LIFE is marked by change. As we experience the changes that occur from childhood to adolescence to adulthood, from marriage and homemaking, from sickness and dying, we are called to greater awareness. Each turn of the wheel offers us the opportunity for spiritual transformation. These life passages inevitably involve a change of consciousness that requires us to learn new behaviors. At times these changes may involve pain, confusion, or ambivalence as old identities die within us and new ones emerge. But the call to change is insistent.

This chapter of *Life Prayers* is divided into eight sections, each marking a major life transition:

Birth

Coming of Age

Courtship

Marriage Vows and Blessings

Healing Prayers

Midlife

Growing Older

Death

The voices in these sections encourage us to embrace the mystery of life's unfoldment, no matter how difficult that may be. They help us cross the threshold into the unknown with humor and acceptance.

As we search our spiritual traditions for meaningful ways to mark personal changes and celebrate rites of passage, many of us are taking the role of minister or priest into our own hands. We are practicing the art of self-generated ceremony. We are writing our own marriage vows, creating initiations for our sons and daughters, and celebrating our midlife or the new kind of work that elderhood brings. With our families and friends, we are creating informal communities of shared experience and mutual commitment.

The prayers in this chapter can help you create these ceremonial moments for yourself, your family, or your friends. They can enable you to explore your own authentic ritual leadership and to fill the initiation you wish to mark with your own values, myths, and symbols.

Releasing the separate one
  is a difficult knot.
Finding yourself is something
  only you can do.
Imagine yourself coming back
  10 years from today
Through time, to help you
  where you must now be.

—Jim Cohn

Self-generated rites of passage help to uncover the meaning implicit in a particular human situation. They give psychological and spiritual power to our new roles. They help these transitions to happen less painfully and more consciously. At their best they provide a deepened appreciation for the unfamiliar and the unexpected. A rite of passage ceremony celebrates a transition such as coming of age or moving into a new home that might otherwise have been simply endured or even ignored and reveals its sacred context.

Through marking critical changes in our life we also indicate to the rest of our community that something significant has happened. In this way such rituals are also social practices, involving the community that witnesses the transformation that is occurring. This provides social consensus for the individual's change in status, increasing the initiate's commitment to his or her new role. In effect, the community is saying someone among us has changed and now needs to be supported differently in day-to-day social interactions. The following prayer for entering spiritual elderhood is an example of the vital role of the community in marking the initiation:

> Eternal wisdom, source of our being,
> and center of all our longing,
> in you our sister has lived to a strong age:
> a woman of dignity and wit,
> in loving insight now a blessed crone.
> May the phase into which she has entered
> bear the marks of your spirit.

May she ever be borne up
by the fierce and tender love of friends
and by you, most intimate friend;
and clothed in your light,
grow in grace as she advances in years;
for your love's sake. Amen.

—Gail A. Ricciuti

Of course, the prayers and poems of initiation in this chapter
need not be used only in formal rituals. They are reminders—useful
at any time—of the joy, struggle, wisdom, and fleeting nature of the
human journey. Life itself gives us the initiations—we only mark
them with our prayers. But by marking them we agree to take in
the lessons, assume our new roles, and adjust our place within our
community and our world.

Birth

Men and women who are on Earth
You are our creators.
We, the unconceived, beseech you:
Let us have living bread
The builder of our new body.
Let us have pure water
The vitalizer of our blood.
Let us have clean air
So that every breath is a caress.
Let us feel the petals of jasmine and roses
Which are as tender as our skin.

Men and women who are on Earth
You are our creators.
We, the unconceived, beseech you:
Do not give us a world of rage and fear
For our minds will be rage and fear.
Do not give us violence and pollution
For our bodies will be disease and abomination
Let us be wherever we are
Rather than bringing us
Into a tormented self-destroying humanity.

Men and women who are on Earth
You are our creators.
We, the unconceived, beseech you:
If you are ready to love and to be loved,
Invite us to this Earth

Of the Thousand Wonders.
And we will be born
To love and be loved.

—Laura Huxley

in the house with the tortoise chair
   she will give birth to the pearl
      to the beautiful feather

in the house of the goddess who sits on a tortoise
   she will give birth to the necklace of pearls
      to the beautiful feathers we are

there she sits on the tortoise
   swelling to give us birth

on your way on your way
child be on your way to me here
   you whom I made new
come here child come be pearl
   be beautiful feather

—Aztec prayer
(English version by Anselm Hollo)

We bless this child with the elements of our common being, with earth, air, fire and water.

(The speaker lifts a handful of earth before the child)

With earth, which is as solid as your given frame, my child, we bless you. Take care of yourself as a body, be good to yourself, for you are a good gift.

(The speaker blows gently on the child's head)

With air, which is as fluctuating as your given passion my child, we bless you. You will know sorrow and joy, rage and contentment, resentment and ecstasy. Feel your passions my child, they are good gifts.

(The speaker holds a flame aloft before the child's eyes)

With fire, which is as illuminating as your given intelligence my child, we bless you. Reason with care, test the world, think with care, for your mind is as good gift.

(The speaker dips fingers into warm water and touches them to the crown of the child's head)

With water, which is as clear as your spirit, my child, we bless you. Grow in conscience, be rooted in good stories, grow spiritually, for spirit too is a good gift.

—Mark Belletini

From the heart of Earth, by means of yellow pollen
    blessing is extended.
From the Heart of Sky, by means of blue pollen
    blessing is extended.
On top of a pollen floor
    may I there in blessing give birth!
On top of a floor of fabrics
    may I there in blessing give birth!
As collected water flows ahead of it,
    whereby blessing moves along ahead of it,
    may I there in blessing give birth!
Thereby without hesitating,
    thereby with its mind straightened,
    thereby with its travel means straightened,
    thereby without its sting,
    may I there in blessing give birth!
As water's child glows behind it
    whereby blessing moves along behind it
    may I there in blessing give birth!
Thereby without hesitating,
    thereby with its mind straightened,
    thereby with its travel means straightened,
    thereby without its sting,
    may I there in blessing give birth!
With pollen moving around it, with blessing
    extending from it by means of pollen,
    may I in blessing give birth!

May I give birth to Pollen Boy,
　　may I give birth to Cornbeetle Boy,
　　may I give birth to Long-life Boy,
　　may I give birth to Happiness Boy!
With long life-happiness surrounding me
　　may I in blessing give birth!
　　May I quickly give birth!
In blessing may I arise again,
　　in blessing may I recover,
　　as one who is long-life-happiness may I live on!
Before me may it be blessed,
　　behind me may it be blessed, below me may it be blessed,
　　above me may it be blessed, in all my surroundings may it be
　　blessed,
may my speech be blessed!
　　It has become blessed again, it has become blessed again,
　　it has become blessed again, it has become blessed again!
　　　　　　　　　　　　　—Navaho birth chant

189

Come to term the started child shocks
Peace upon me; I am great with peace;
Pain teaches primal cause; my bones unlock
To learn my final end. The formal increase
Of passionate patience breaks into a storm of heat
Where calling on you love my heart's hopes rise
With violence to seize as prayer this sweet
Submitting act. I pray. Loud with surprise
Thrown sprung back wide the blithe body lies
Exultant and wise. The born child cries.
                                        —Marie Ponsot

Here am I,
myself,
but also vessel of creation.

Rhythms of the ages
stir the Womb of Woman,
my own womb—
ancient pulse in my own heartbeat,
nourishment in my own breast.
This life through me
was fathered deep
in fire-consecrated flesh,
and here, behold!
A miracle,
that what was not before
is
now!

—Nancy Rose Meeker

I cut the cord
Those scissors in hand
We are no longer
the same

Praise a Lord!
Un hijo, a Son, a Boy!
Two more feet touch the earth!
—Joe Richey

That she was taken out of her mother,
 thanks be for that!
That she, the little one,
 was taken out of her, we say,
 thanks be for that!
—West Greenland Eskimo song

At your birth, my daughter
I heard you cry
a lamb unblemished
my new offering
to the world.
—Amelia Blossom House

Rise up, child of earth
Let life rise up in you,
full-term, new-born.
Time enough in wondrous darkness,
Echoed sounds of voices, stirrings,
splashings of new life.
Relinquish to memory this one mystery
we yearn to know and will again
in after-death.
So much latent
still to rise
Until our rising lifts us to a depth
that questions every truth
we've ever known.

193

Mud-stirred of first-clay.
Plaything of a potter who fell in love
with her hands' work.
Blessed be her handiwork.
Blessed be the work of her hands.
Blessed be.

—Pat Kozak

Give heed, my child, lift your eyes,
behold the one who is standing here,
Behold, my child! waiting now to fit
and set you here apart.
Give heed, my child. Look!
Sacred ointment now is here come to you.

Give heed, my child, lift your eyes,
behold the one who has holy made.
Behold, my child! You are set apart,
and finished is the task.
Give heed, my child. Look!
Sacred ointment now has set you apart.

—Pawnee song

Newborn, on the naked sand
Nakedly lay it.
Next to the earth mother,
That it may know her;
Having good thoughts of her, the food giver.

Newborn, we tenderly
In our arms take it,
Making good thoughts.
House-god, be entreated,
That it may grow from childhood to manhood,
Happy, contented;
Beautifully walking
The trail to old age.
Having good thoughts of the earth its mother,
That she may give it the fruits of her being.

Newborn, on the naked sand
Nakedly lay it.

—Grand Pueblos prayer

Earth Goddess, hear.
We shall give birth to sons.
Earth Goddess, hear.
We shall give birth to daughters.
Earth Goddess, hear.
We shall train them.
Earth Goddess, hear.
When we are old they will feed us.
Earth Goddess, hear.
Whoever sees us with an evil eye,
When he plants may the floods sweep his mounds away.
Whoever wishes us evil,
May he break his fist on the ground.
We are broody hens, we have chicks.
We do not fly up,
We look after our brood.
We do not eye others with an evil eye.
This big-headed thing that came home yesterday,
He is yet a seed.
If you wish that he germinates
And grows to be a tree,
We shall be ever thankful.
Earth Goddess, hear;
He will grow to be like his stock.

       —Igbo prayer, Nigeria

When the child is born, the afterbirth is taken and offered to a young tree or to a greasewood bush. The
child becomes rooted in the Earth, and when it is
born the roots are like a little string. Our rootedness
to the Earth is like tying a string to yourself and the
other end to your mother. The string thickens with
each Offering, with each ceremony, each member of
the family, each generation.

—Lenora Hatathlie Hill, Navajo

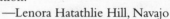

The placenta must be buried with ceremony in the
compound with the witch-doctor present. As the
navel cord ties an unborn child to the womb, so does
the buried cord tie the child to the land, to the sacred
earth of the tribe, to the Great Mother Earth. If the
child ever leaves the place he will come home again
because the tug of this cord will always pull him towards his own.

When I go home I shall stand on the spot where
the waiting ones stood that night [of my birth] in the
storm and I shall speak these words: "My belly is this
day reunited with the belly of my Great Mother,
Earth!"

—Prince Modupe, Guinea

My sun!
My morning star!
Help this child to become a man.
I name him
Rain-dew Falling!
I name him
Star Mountain!

—Tewa prayer

Animals that move on the surface, animals under ground
that inhabit the water, listen, be attentive. This one
standing here asks of you a name that is good.

—Arapaho prayer

Coming of Age

Tomorrow the drums will beat and I will
dance my last dance as a child.
The beating drums will sound here and
the echoes will reach Nimba—
My footsteps will echo on the hollow
ground and keep time with the drums.
My body will be washed and the white chalk
will run down and sink into the ground
with my footsteps—
And the drums will beat, and we all will dance.
Being a child is over—and I must start the
dance of womanhood—while the drums beat out my
    life.

—Alice Perry Johnson

201

Releasing the separate one
  is a difficult knot.

Finding yourself is something
  only you can do.

Imagine yourself coming back
  10 years from today

Through time, to help you
  where you must now be.

—Jim Cohn

We bathe your palms
   In showers of wine,
In the crook of the kindling,
   In the seven elements,
In the sap of the tree,
   In the milk of honey,

We place nine pure, choice gifts
   In your clear beloved face:

The gift of form,
   The gift of voice,
The gift of fortune,
   The gift of goodness,
The gift of eminence,
   The gift of charity,
The gift of integrity,
   The gift of true nobility,
The gift of apt speech.
                    —Traditional Gaelic

Initiations: Coming of Age

Power of raven be yours,
Power of eagle be yours,
Power of the *Fianna*.

Power of storm be yours,
Power of moon be yours,
Power of sun.

Power of sea be yours,
Power of land be yours,
Power of heaven.

Goodness of sea be yours,
Goodness of earth be yours,
Goodness of heaven.

Each day be joy to you,
No day be sad to you,
Honour and tenderness.
—Mary Mackintosh

Lord of the Mountain,
Reared within the Mountain
Young Man, Chieftain,
Here's a young man's prayer!
Hear a prayer for cleanness.
Keeper of the strong rain,
Drumming on the mountain;
Lord of the small rain
That restores the earth in newness;
Keeper of the clean rain,
Hear a prayer for wholeness,

Young Man, Chieftain,
Hear a prayer for fleetness.
Keeper of the deer's way,
Reared among the eagles,
Clear my feet of slothness.
Keeper of the paths of men,
Hear a prayer for straightness.

Hear a prayer for courage.
Lord of the thin peaks,
Reared amid the thunder;
Keeper of the headlands
Holding up the harvest,
Keeper of the strong rocks
Hear a prayer for staunchness.

Young Man, Chieftain,
Spirit of the Mountain!

—Navajo prayer

Initiations: Coming of Age

Hold out.
Take only the worthy guest.
You are the guardian.
you the sacred host,
your body the temple.
Keep your sanctuary safe.
Receive no one without
deep mutual welcome.

Take in only angels—
those sent by God
bearing messages
of recognition—
    I see you, entire,
    complete, wholly—
    all suffering,
    all goodness,
    all power,
    all mirth.
    Bright radiance inside,
    and the silence, the darkness.

Such ones as can speak these words
will inspire you to conceive
and help you to give birth
to the divine child.

In your union God sees
and becomes one with
Godself in each lover.

Between the legs of your dance
is the Gate of Heaven. It waits
for the true lover to enter
and create the union
of Heaven and Earth.

This communion of sex
is no sweet foretaste
but already participation,
enactment of Heaven,
the best there is from God.

You were born for this.
Do not say yes to less
than two loving fullnesses
overflowing into pure bliss . . .
—Alla Renée Bozarth

Please bring strange things.
Please come bringing new things.
Let very old things come into your hands.
Let what you do not know come into your eyes.
Let desert sand harden your feet.
Let the arch of your feet be the mountains.
Let the paths of your fingertips be your maps
and the ways you go be the lines on your palms.
Let there be deep snow in your inbreathing
and your outbreath be the shining of ice.
May your mouth contain the shapes of strange words.
May you smell food cooking you have not eaten.
May the spring of a foreign river be your navel.
May your soul be at home where there are no houses.
Walk carefully, well loved one,
walk mindfully, well loved one,
walk fearlessly, well loved one.
Return with us, return to us,
be always coming home.

—Ursula K. Le Guin

Be not too wise, nor too foolish,
be not too conceited, nor too diffident,
be not too haughty, nor too humble,
be not too talkative, nor too silent,
be not too hard, nor too feeble,
for:
If you be too wise, one will expect too much of you;
if you be foolish, you will be deceived;
if you be too conceited, you will be thought vexatious;
if you be too humble, you will be without honour;
if you be too talkative, you will not be heeded;
if you be too silent, you will not be regarded;
if you be too hard, you will be broken;
if you be too feeble, you will be crushed.

—Cormac

209

If you open it, close it.
If you turn it on, turn it off.
If you unlock it, lock it up.
If you break it, admit it.
If you can't fix it, call in someone who can.
If you borrow it, return it.
If you value it, take care of it.
If you make a mess, clean it up.
If you move it, put it back.
If it belongs to someone else and you want to use it,
    get permission.
If you don't know how to operate it, leave it alone.
If it's none of your business, don't ask questions.
If it ain't broke, don't fix it.
If it will brighten someone's day, say it!

—Anonymous

If you can keep your head when all about you
    Are losing theirs and blaming it on you,
If you can trust yourself when all men doubt you,
    But make allowance for their doubting too;
If you can wait and not be tired by waiting
    Or being lied about, don't deal in lies,
Or being hated don't give way to hating
    And yet don't look too good, nor talk too wise:

If you can dream—and not make dreams your master;
    If you can think—and not make thoughts your aim:
If you can meet with Triumph and Disaster
    And treat those two impostors just the same;
If you can bear to hear the truth you've spoken
    Twisted by knaves to make a trap for fools,
Or watch the things you gave your life to, broken,
    And stoop and build 'em up with worn-out tools:

If you can make one heap of all your winnings
    And risk it on one turn of pitch-and-toss,
And lose, and start again at your beginnings
And never breathe a word about your loss;
If you can force your heart and nerve and sinew
    To serve your turn long after they are gone,
And so hold on when there is nothing in you
    Except the Will which says to them: "Hold on!"

Initiations: Coming of Age

If you can talk with crowds and keep your virtue,
    Or walk with Kings—nor lose the common touch,
If neither foes nor loving friends can hurt you,
    If all men count with you, but none too much;
If you can fill the unforgiving minute
    With sixty seconds' worth of distance run,
Yours is the Earth and everything that's in it,
    And—which is more—you'll be a Man, my son!
                                —Rudyard Kipling

Go placidly amid the noise and haste, and remember what peace there may be in silence. As far as possible without surrender be on good terms with all persons. Speak your truth quietly and clearly; and listen to others, even the dull and ignorant; they too have their story. Avoid loud and aggressive persons, they are vexatious to the spirit. If you compare yourself with others, you may become vain and bitter; for always there will be greater and lesser persons than yourself. Enjoy your achievements as well as your plans.

Keep interested in your own career, however humble, it is a real possession in the changing fortunes of time. Exercise caution in your business affairs; for the world is full of trickery. But let this not blind you to what virtue there is; many persons strive for high ideals; and everywhere life is full of heroism. Be yourself. Especially, do not feign affection. Neither be cynical about love; for in the face of all aridity and disenchantment it is perennial as the grass.

Take kindly the counsel of the years, gracefully surrendering the things of youth. Nurture strength of spirit to shield you in sudden misfortune. But do not distress yourself with imaginings. Many fears are born of fatigue and loneliness. Beyond a wholesome discipline, be gentle with yourself.

You are a child of the universe, no less than the trees and the stars; you have a right to be here . . .

Whatever your labors and aspirations, in the noisy confusion of life keep peace with your soul. With all its shame, drudgery and broken dreams, it is still a beautiful world. Be cheerful. Strive to be happy.

—Seventeenth-century anonymous

214

May there always be work for your hands to do
May your purse always hold a coin or two
May the sun always shine upon your window pane
May a rainbow be certain to follow each rain
May the hand of a friend always be near to you and
May God fill your heart with gladness to cheer you.

—Irish blessing

Hold on to what is good
even if it is
a handful of earth.
Hold on to what you believe
even if it is
a tree which stands by itself.
Hold on to what you must do
even if it is
a long way from here.
Hold on to life even when
it is easier letting go.
Hold on to my hand even when
I have gone away from you.

—Nancy Wood

215

If you have time to chatter
Read books
If you have time to read
Walk into mountain, desert and ocean
If you have time to walk
sing songs and dance
If you have time to dance
Sit quietly, you Happy Lucky Idiot
—Nanao Sakaki

Do not seek too much fame,
but do not seek obscurity.
Be proud.
But do not remind the world of your deeds.
Excel when you must,
but do not excel the world.
Many heroes are not yet born,
many have already died.
To be alive to hear this song is a victory.
—West African song

Have patience with everything unresolved in your heart
and try to love the questions themselves . . .
Don't search for the answers,
which could not be given to you now,
because you would not be able to live them.
And the point is, to live everything.
Live the questions now.
Perhaps then, someday far in the future,
you will gradually, without even noticing it,
live your way into the answer.

—Rainer Maria Rilke

You are going for a long time
and nobody knows what to expect

we are trying to learn
not to accompany gifts with advice

or to suppose that we can protect you
from being changed

by something that we do not know
but have always turned away from

even by the sea that we love
with its breaking

and the dissolving days
and the shadows on the wall

together we look at the young trees
we read the news we smell the morning

we cannot tell you what to take with you
in your light baggage

—W. S. Merwin

Courtship

This is the truth, my lover:
My childhood could not last;
Since my long hair was clipped
Full eight long years have passed.
Blooming like a fruit tree,
I am a secret stream
Running beneath earth's surface
And you my constant dream.
I, too, have prayed the gods
To make my childhood stay.
But time must take its course
And love will have its way.
                    —Anonymous Japanese

221

He called her: golden dawn
She called him: the wind whistles

He called her: heart of the sky
She called him: message bringer

He called her: mother of pearl
   barley woman, rice provider,
   millet basket, corn maid,
   flax princess, all-maker, weef

She called him: fawn, roebuck,
   stag, courage, thunderman,
   all-in-green, mountain strider,
   keeper of forests, my-love-rides

He called her: the tree is
She called him: bird dancing

He called her: who stands,
   has stood, will always stand
She called him: arriver

He called her: the heart and the womb
   are similar
She called him: arrow in my heart.

           —Judy Grahn

Wake, sons, lovers,
young chiefs, hunters with arrows!
Sharpen the darts, make string, bend the bow;
Keen, keen as light,
and clear as the wind be your eyes!
The women await you in secret places,
They have hidden themselves in the leafy shelters:
All the green leagues of the forest
are ashake with invitation.
The quick beating of their hearts
is the whisper along the bending grass.
The sod grows warm—O men,
Summer-dawn is the spirit of the women!
                            —Constance Lindsay Skinner

223

Come, come, O swift and strong!
We are the women: seek us!
Our hearts, like little swallows,
    nest above the secret pools.
Oh, say, shall not the winged dart pierce,
And the shadow of the bended bow
Stir the still, deep pools?
Oh, the waters shall sparkle and leap and mingle,
And brim at your lips, O men!
They shall be poured out and drip upon a chief's feet;
They shall fill the hollows of his house with children!
Flowing in laughter and whispers and little cries
As smoke through the smoke-hole at evening!
Ai! ah! ai! Women! Waken the soil with freshets;
Bear joy upward as a canoe with sails,
    swifter than paddles.
O men, hunters of life,
We are the harborers, the foresters—the women:
Seek us!

—Constance Lindsay Skinner

I hunger to engage!
Your eyes,
your mouth,
your thought!
In intercourse of word
or flesh
I know you,
and to you
am known.

Come be with me in dappled sunlight,
languorous in laughter shared.
O come explore delicious realms
and let our sacred touch
go deep.

I dance the earth and sky ecstatic,
bodies singing,
rhythms hot!
Your pleasured smile is holy wine,
eyes closed,
breath caught.

The moment is our crucible,
luminous with reverent flame—
creative juices, honey-sweet,
go incandescent,
raised to heaven,
offered in your name.

—Nancy Rose Meeker

I want you when the shades of eve are falling
    And purple shadows drift across the land;
When sleepy birds to loving mates are calling—
    I want the soothing softness of your hand.

I want you when the stars shine up above me,
    And Heaven's flooded with the bright moonlight;
I want you with your arms and lips to love me
    Throughout the wonder watches of the night.

I want you when in dreams I still remember
    The ling'ring of your kiss—for old times' sake—
With all your gentle ways, so sweetly tender,
    I want you in the morning when I wake.

I want you when the day is at its noontime,
    Sun-steeped and quiet, or drenched with sheets of rain;
I want you when the roses bloom in June-time;
    I want you when the violets come again.

I want you when my soul is thrilled with passion;
    I want you when I'm weary and depressed;
I want you when in lazy, slumbrous fashion
    My senses need the haven of your breast.

I want you when through field and wood I'm roaming;
    I want you when I'm standing on the shore;
I want you when the summer birds are homing—
    And when they've flown—I want you more and more.

I want you, dear, through every changing season;
    I want you with a tear or with a smile;
I want you more than any rhyme or reason—
    I want you, want you, want you—all the while.
                    —Arthur L. Gillom

My sweetheart
   a long time
   I have been waiting for you
   to come over
      where I am.

              —Chippewa song

In an accessible place
you will sleep.
At midnight
I will come.

              —Inca song

Whomsoe'er look I upon
   He becomes love-crazed;
Whomsoe'er speak I unto,
   He becomes love-crazed;
Whomsoe'er whisper I to,
   He becomes love-crazed;
All men who love women,
Them I rule, them I rule,
   My friend;
Whom I touch, whom I touch,
   He becomes love-crazed.

          —Winnebago love song

229

Ruda! Ruda!
O you who dwell in the skies,
Who love the rain—
O you who dwell in the skies!
Make it be that he will find
   all other women unattractive.
Let him think of me,
When the sun disappears in the west.

          —Anambe prayer

The voice of my love: listen!
bounding over the mountains
toward me, across the hills.

My love is a gazelle, a wild stag.
There he stands on the other side
of our wall, gazing
between the stones.

And he calls to me:
Hurry, my love, my friend,
and come away!

Look, winter is over,
the rains are done,
wildflowers spring up in the fields.
Now is the time of the nightingale.
In every meadow you hear
the song of the turtledove.

The fig tree has sweetened
its new green fruit
and the young budded vines smell spicey.
Hurry, my love, my friend
come away.

My love in the clefts of the rock
in the shadow of the cliff,

let me see you, all of you!
Let me hear your voice,
your delicious song.
I love to look at you.

> —The Song of Songs
> (translated by Ariel and Chana Bloch)

Wild nights! Wild nights!
Were I with thee,
Wild nights should be
Our Luxury!

Futile the winds
To a heart in port,—
Done with the compass,
Done with the chart.

Rowing in Eden!
Ah! the sea!
Might I but moor
To-night in thee!

> —Emily Dickinson

The sweet soul is sexual, we say
lost in each other, what he called
the id is so much more and
no object in the universe travels faster
than the speed of light, we whisper,
love, this motion of light
does not change, I see it
in the saying of it to you,
I hear it in your hearing
your hands find me saying
yes, how everything,
I could die, fits together,
and the sweet soul
is so large, so large, and hold
me so that bone bursts upon bone
and this is the bone of your face
I say astonished and let me be
possessed by astonishment
of you, your being and the history
of your bright speech breaking in me
as light on every distant feeling
the story of how you came here
evokes to fullness in me, taste
and take into your mouth, love, this sweetness
your sweetness you have made in me,
we say, shuddering, delight.

—Susan Griffin

I watch you
from the gentle slope
where it is warm
by your shoulder.
My eyes are closed.
I can feel the tap
of your blood
against my cheek.
Inside my mind,
I see the gentle move
ment of your valleys,
the undulations
of slow turnings.
Opening my eyes,
there is a soft dark
and beautiful butte
moving up and down
as you breathe.
There are fine
and very tiny ferns
growing, and I can
make them move
by breathing.
I watch you with my skin
moving upon yours,
and I have known you well.
—Simon Ortiz

233

Jasmine unfolding, the scent and color attracting the bees,
     the darker veins guiding them toward the nectar,
honey in honeycombs, worms aerating soil,
       the levity of bird bones,
     fins of fish, the eye blinking—
who could have ever conceived it?
 the crescent moon, tender as new love in the luminescent blue,
milkweed silk—who could have imagined it?

And my lover, when she lifts her lips to me
        and I first feel that softness
   warm like summer nights as a child
when she rubs against me like fur
and small cries escape my mouth like birds,
"Sing to me," she breathes
and I sing glory I did not know was mine to sing.

What is this but a miracle?
What is this but the improbable, marvelous reward of desire?

Desire—that fire I was taught to suspect,
     that intensity I struggled to calm.
"Don't want too much," the voices warned.

234

No. Want. Want life.
Want this fragile oasis of the galaxy to flourish.

Want fertility, want seasons, want this spectacular
    array of creatures,
this brilliant balance of need.

Want it. Want it all.
Desire. Welcome her raging power.
May her strength course through us.
Desire, she is life. Desire life.
Allow ourselves to desire life, to want this sweetness
so passionately, that we live for it.

—Ellen Bass

235

Blessed are the man and the woman
   who have grown beyond their greed
   and have put an end to their hatred
   and no longer nourish illusions.
But they delight in the way things are
   and keep their hearts open, day and night.
They are like trees planted near flowing rivers,
   which bear fruit when they are ready.
Their leaves will not fall or wither.
   Everything they do will succeed.
            —Psalm 1 (version by Stephen Mitchell)

Thank you, my dear

You came, and you did
well to come: I needed
you. You have made

love blaze up in
my breast—bless you!
Bless you as often

as the hours have
been endless to me
while you were gone

            —Sappho

Marriage Vows
and Blessings

May these vows and this marriage be blessed.
May it be sweet milk,
this marriage, like wine and halvah.
May this marriage offer fruit and shade
like the date palm.
May this marriage be full of laughter,
our every day a day in paradise.
May this marriage be a sign of compassion,
a seal of happiness here and hereafter.
May this marriage have a fair face and a good name,
an omen as welcome
as the moon in a clear blue sky.
I am out of words to describe
how spirit mingles in this marriage.

—Rumi

We invoke you, Goddess of Life, by these roots,
so that this relationship may be deeply rooted in the community
and in the two who are joining their lives today.

We invoke thee by the stems and branches,
that this alliance may reach out to others
and gather a rich community around it.

We invoke thee by flowers,
that this relationship may make
the respective talents and desires of both partners grow.

We invoke thee by the seeds,
that this love may create new love
and our devotion bring forth new discoveries in each other.
—Zsuzsanna E. Budapest

1. Blessed be the One who created the fruit of the vine. Bless the two of you who come out of long traditions of struggling to find out what it is to be human, may you be full of the wine of life, may the life force and the knowledge of the human heart be with you.

2. Blessed be the Gods. All creation mirrors your splendor and reflects your radiance. Bless the two of you. May you know that all beauty comes from The Great Heart and may you live in its radiance.

3. Blessed be the Divine Spirit who created human beings. Bless the two of you. May you know it all—joy and struggle, beauty and sorrow, sweat, tears, solitude, companionship, laughter and ecstasy. May your marriage be strong enough to support you to experience whatever you must as you come to know yourselves and each other and to discover the entire range of your humanity in the process of soul making.

4. Blessed be the Ones who created Woman and Man in the divine image, so we may live, love and perpetuate life. Bless the two of you. May you delight in the wondrousness and impossibility of the fact that you are so similar and so different—may the difficulty and the enormous pleasure of being a man and woman continually fascinate and engage you and be the source of your bonding.

5. Blessed be the Holy Ones who rejoice with the People in their Joy. It is said that everyone gets married at a wedding. Blessed be the two of you who bring us together through your union.

6. Blessed be the Holy Ones who rejoice that the love between this woman and this man is the very first love between the first man and the first woman in the Garden. Blessed be the two of you who recreate the world for us and for yourselves. May your love be as old and as new as the first love, and may you also bring new life, in all its forms, into the world.

7. Blessed be the Divine Spirit. Joy and Gladness. Man and Woman. Mirth and Exultation. Pleasure and Delight. Love and Friendship. Peace and Community between all peoples. Blessed be the two of you; may you live in the spirit and in the heart.

—Deena Metzger

We call upon all that we hold most sacred to

Bless this marriage

We call upon the earth, our planet home, with its beautiful depths and soaring heights, its vitality and abundance of life, and together we ask that it

Bless this marriage

We call upon the mountains, the green mountains and the white, and the high valleys and meadows filled with wild flowers, the snows that never melt, the summits of intense silence, and we ask that they

Bless this marriage

We call upon the waters that rim the earth, horizon to horizon, that flow in our rivers and streams, that fall upon our gardens and fields, that fill our ponds and pools, and we ask that they

Bless this marriage

We call upon the land which grows our food, the nurturing soil, the fertile fields, the abundant gardens and orchards, and we ask that they

Bless this marriage

We call upon the forests, the great trees reaching to the sky with earth in their roots and heaven in their branches, the fir and the pine, the cedar and the maple, and we ask them to

Bless this marriage

We call upon the moon and the stars and the sun, who govern the rhythms and seasons of our lives and remind us that we are part of a great and wondrous universe, and we ask them to

Bless this marriage

We call upon all those who have lived on this earth, our ancestors and our friends, who dreamed the best for future generations, and upon whose lives our lives are built, and with thanksgiving, we call upon them to

Bless this marriage

We call upon the family and friends and all those who love and cherish and sustain this couple, and ask that together we

Bless this marriage

And lastly, we call upon the power and presence of the Christ, on that which asks us to become greater than ourselves so that the one may become two and the two may become one, and all together we

Bless this marriage!

—Fritz Hull

Brother and Sister, please kneel down. Noble community, please listen. This is the moment when our Brother and Sister will make the vow to practice the Five Awarenesses. Students of the Buddha are aware that life is one and that happiness is not an individual matter. By living and practicing awareness, we bring peace and joy to our lives and the lives of those who are related to us. Brother and Sister, please repeat the Five Awarenesses after me, and say yes, firmly, if you intend to make the vow to practice them. After each awareness, when you hear the sound of the bell, bow deeply to the Three Jewels.

The First Awareness

We are aware that all generations of our ancestors and all future generations are present in us.

This is the first of the Five Awarenesses. Do you make the vow to receive, study, and practice it? *(Bell)*

The Second Awareness

We are aware of the expectations that our ancestors, our children, and their children have of us.

This is the second of the five awarenesses. Do you make the vow to receive, study, and practice it? *(Bell)*

The Third Awareness

We are aware that our joy, peace, freedom, and harmony are the joy, peace, freedom, and harmony of our ancestors, our children, and their children.

This is the third of the Five Awarenesses. Do you make the vow to receive, study, and practice it? *(Bell)*

The Fourth Awareness

We are aware that understanding is the very foundation of love.

This is the fourth of the Five Awarenesses. Do you make the vow to receive, study, and practice it? *(Bell)*

The Fifth Awareness

We are aware that blaming and arguing never help us and only create a wider gap between us, that only understanding, trust, and love can help us change and grow.

This is the fifth of the Five Awarenesses. Do you make the vow to receive, study, and practice it? *(Bell)*

—Thich Nhat Hanh

May the Great Spirit send his choicest gifts to you
May the Sun father and Moon mother
shed their softest beams on you
May the four winds of heaven glow gently upon you
and upon those with whom you share your heart and home.
—Coahuila blessing

May the blessing of God go before you.
May Her grace and peace abound.
May Her Spirit live within you.
May her love wrap you 'round.
May Her blessing remain with you always.
May you walk on holy ground.
—Miriam Therese Winter

Initiations: Marriage Vows and Blessings

United your resolve, united your hearts,
    may your spirits be at one,
that you may long together dwell
    in unity and concord.
                —Rig Veda (the final mantra)

May your love be firm,
and may your dream of life together
be a river between two shores—
by day bathed in sunlight, and by night
illuminated from within.
May the heron carry news of you to the heavens,
and the salmon bring the sea's blue grace.
May your twin thoughts spiral upward like leafy vines,
like fiddle strings in the wind,
and be as noble as the Douglas fir.
May you never find yourselves back to back
without love pulling you around
into each other's arms.
                —James Bertolino

Keep your passion alive—
it will warm you when the
world around you grows cold.
It will not allow comfortable
familiarity to rob you of that
special glow that comes with
loving deeply. It can lift
you over stone walls of anger
and carry you across vast
deserts of alienation. But its
greatest gift is that of touch—
for passion cannot dwell in
solitude—it thrives best in
loving embrace. So keep your
passion alive—hold one
another as a tree holds the
Earth and your love will
bear the fruit of many,
many seasons.

    —Shamaan Ochaum Climbing Eagle

That a woman not ask a man to leave meaningful work
                to follow her.
That a man not ask a woman to leave meaningful work
                to follow him.

That no one try to put Eros in bondage.
But that no one put a cudgel in the hands of Eros.

That our loyalty to one another and our loyalty to our work
not be set in false conflict.

That our love for each other give us love for each other's work.
That our love for each other's work give us love for one another.

That our love for each other's work give us love for one another.
That our love for each other give us love for each other's work.

That our love for each other, if need be,
give way to absence. And the unknown.

That we endure absence, if need be,
without losing our love for each other.
Without closing our doors to the unknown.
                             —Denise Levertov

I add my breath to your breath
that our days may be long on the Earth,
That the days of our people may be long,
that we shall be as one person,
that we may finish our road together.

—Laguna Pueblo prayer

I honor your gods
I drink at your well
I bring an undefended heart to our meeting place
I have no cherished outcome
I will not negotiate by withholding
I am not subject to disappointment

—Celtic vow

Standing again
within and among things,
Standing with each other
as sisters and brothers, mothers and fathers,
daughters and sons, grandmothers and grandfathers—
the past and present generations of our people,
Standing again
with and among all items of life;
the land, rivers, the mountains, plants, animals,
all life that is around us
that we are included with,
Standing within the circle of the horizon,
the day sky and the night sky,
the sun, moon, the cycle of seasons
and the earth mother which sustains us,
Standing again
with all things
that have been in the past,
that are in the present,
and that will be in the future
we acknowledge ourselves
to be in a relationship that is responsible
and proper, that is loving and compassionate,
for the sake of the land and all people;
we ask humbly of the creative forces of life
that we be given a portion
with which to help ourselves so that our struggle

and work will also be creative
for the continuance of life,
Standing again, within, among all things
we ask in all sincerity, for hope, courage, peace,
strength, vision, unity and continuance.

—Simon Ortiz

We swear by peace and love to stand
Heart to heart and hand in hand.
Mark, O Spirit, and hear us now,
Confirming this our Sacred Vow.

—Druidic vow

You and I
Have so much love,
That it
Burns like a fire,
In which we bake a lump of clay
Molded into a figure of you
And a figure of me.
Then we take both of them,
And break them into pieces,
And mix the pieces with water,
And mold again a figure of you,
And a figure of me.
I am in your clay.
You are in my clay.
In life we share a single quilt.
In death we will share one coffin.

—Kuan Tao-sheng

Sweet be the glances we exchange,
our faces showing true concord
Enshrine me in your heart and let
one spirit dwell within us.
I wrap around you this my robe
which came to me from Manu,
so that you may be wholly mine
and never seek another.

I am He, you are She,
I am Song, you are Verse,
I am Heaven, you are Earth.
We two shall here together dwell,
becoming parents of children.
—Atharva Veda VII, 36-37; XIV, 2

I love you,
Not only for what you are,
But for what I am
When I am with you.

I love you,
Not only for what
You have made of yourself,
But for what
You are making of me.

I love you
For the part of me
That you bring out;
I love you
For putting your hand
Into my heaped-up heart
And passing over
All the foolish, weak things
That you can't help
Dimly seeing there,
And for drawing out
Into the light
All the beautiful belongings
That no one else had looked
Quite far enough to find.

I love you because you
Are helping me to make

Of the lumber of my life
Not a tavern
But a temple;
Out of the works
Of my every day
Not a reproach
But a song.

I love you
Because you have done
More than any creed
Could have done
To make me good,
And more than any fate
Could have done
To make me happy.

You have done it
Without a touch,
Without a word,
Without a sign.
You have done it
By being yourself.
Perhaps that is what
Being a friend means,
After all.
                    —Roy Croft

It is for the union of you and me
that there is light in the sky.
It is for the union of you and me
that the earth is decked in dusky green.
It is for the union of you and me
that the night sits motionless with the world in her arms;
dawn appears opening the eastern door
with sweet murmurs in her voice.

The boat of hope sails along the currents of
eternity towards that union,
flowers of the ages are being gathered together
for its welcoming ritual.

It is for the union of you and me
that this heart of mine, in the garb of a bride,
has proceeded from birth to birth
upon the surface of this ever-turning world
to choose the beloved.

—Rabindranath Tagore

Initiations: Marriage Vows and Blessings

You are the star of each night,
You are the brightness of every morning,
You are the story of each guest,
You are the report of every land.

No evil shall befall you,
On hill nor bank,
In field or valley,
On mountain or in glen.

Neither above nor below,
Neither in sea
Nor on shore,
In skies above,
Nor in the depths.

You are the kernel of my heart,
You are the face of my sun,
You are the harp of my music,
You are the crown of my company.

—Carmina Gadelica

You are a shade in the heat,
  You are a shelter in the cold,
You are eyes to the blind,
  You are a staff to the pilgrim,
You are an island in the sea,
  You are a stronghold upon land,
You are a well in the wasteland,
  You are healing to the sick.

You are the luck of every joy,
  You are the light of the sun's beams,
You are the door of lordly welcome,
  You are the pole star of guidance,
You are the step of the roe of the height,
  You are the step of the white-faced mare,
You are the grace of the swimming swan,
  You are the jewel in each mystery.

—Gaelic prayer

God of mercy,
God of grace,
Be pleased to bless
This dwelling place.
May peace and kindly deeds
Be found;
May gratitude and love
Abound.

—Norma Woodbridge

Lord, behold our family here assembled.
We thank you for this place in which we dwell,
for the love that unites us,
for the peace accorded us this day,
for the hope with which we expect the morrow;
for the health, the work, the food and the bright skies
that make our lives delightful;
for our friends in all parts of the earth. Amen

—Robert Louis Stevenson

May the door of this home be wide enough
to receive all who hunger for love,
all who are lonely for friendship.
May it welcome all who have cares to unburden,
thanks to express, hopes to nurture.
May the door of this house be narrow enough
to shut out pettiness and pride, envy and enmity.
May its threshold be no stumbling block
to young or strained feet.
May it be too high to admit complacency,
selfishness and harshness.
May this home be for all who enter,
the doorway to richness and a more meaningful life.
                    —The Siddur of Shir Chadash

A blessing upon your new home,
  A blessing upon your new hearth,
A blessing upon your new dwelling,
  Upon your newly kindled fire.

A blessing upon your tallest grass,
  A blessing upon your fruitful partner,
A blessing upon your growing son/s,
  Upon your growing daughter/s.

A blessing upon the household's helpers,
  A blessing upon the children yet unborn,
A blessing upon the wise parents,
  Upon your occupation.

A blessing upon your goods and income,
  A blessing upon your kith and kin,
A blessing upon you in light or darkness,
  Each day and night of your lives.

             —Carmina Gadelica

Dwell in this home; never be parted!
Enjoy the full duration of your days,
with sons and grandsons playing to the end,
rejoicing in your home to your heart's content.

             —Rig Veda x, 42

Healing Prayers

O Earth, wrap me
in your leaves—
heal me.

Let me fall
on your Earthbreast—
feed me.

Sing to me
under the round nests
in your cedar trees.

Embrace me
when I sleep
in your shade.

Let your eye keep me
protected and cool—
hide me.

Warm me
with naked summer
kisses and

Cloister me
around
with wildflowers.

Refresh me
with springs
and living waters.

Draw me down
into your well
of rebirth and

Let my wounds
open
and empty

Into your wonderful
compost
heap.

Then fill me
with your fruit
and bread, start over,

Let my wounds
become fertile
gardens and

Let me be,
let me live
again.
            —Alla Renée Bozarth

266

Oh, you of wounded spirits,
I offer you a place of rest;
Walk among my mountains,
And climb to Eagle's nest.
Come swim my oceans,
Or feel my desert's fire.
Sit beside running waters
To reclaim your heart's desire.
Seek my silent forests,
Or walk my open plains,
Travel the deepest jungles
'Til you hear my love's refrain.
I am always waiting
To allow each child to heal,
To cradle the wounded spirits,
And teach them how to feel.
I am the Earth Mother,
Who loves without regret,
Tending all my children,
Who through tears
    have paid all debts.

—Jamie Sams

I am the child of the universe.
She puts her almighty protection around me.
I am free from accidents, death, sickness.
I am now shining with golden light from top to toe.
I am her chosen protected child, and she is my shield.
The winds shall aid my progress.
Water shall cleanse me from fear,
Fire will purify my doubts,
And the earth shall nourish me to health.
All is well, all is well, all is well.

—Zsuzsanna E. Budapest

There are moments when wellness escapes us,
moments when pain and suffering
are not dim possibilities
but all too agonizing realities.
At such moments we must open ourselves to healing.

Much we can do for ourselves;
and what we can do
we must do—
healing,
no less than illness,
is participatory.

But even when we do all we can do
there is,
often,
still much left to be done.
And so we turn as well to our healers
seeking their skill to aid in our struggle for wellness.

But even when they do all they can do
there is,
often,
still much left to be done.
And so we turn to Life,
to the vast Power of Being that animates the universe
as the ocean animates the wave,
seeking to let go of that which blocks our healing.

Life Prayers

May those
whose lives are gripped in the palm of suffering
open
even now
to the Wonder of Life.
May they let go of the hurt
and Meet the True Self beyond pain,
the Uncarved Block
that is our joyous Unity with Holiness.

May they discover through pain and torment
the strength to live with grace and humor.
May they discover through doubt and anguish
the strength to live with dignity and holiness.
May they discover through suffering and fear
the strength to move toward healing.

—Rabbi Rami M. Shapiro

O
body!
for 41 years
1,573 experts with
14,355 combined years of training
have failed
to
cure your
wounds.

Deep inside
I
am
whole

—Rachel Naomi Remen

I accept the cancer in this body,
Knowing that it is not me.
Hand in hand we play and practice together,
That all who suffer may be free.

—Annabel Laity

You carry the cure within you.
Everything that comes your way is blessed.
The Creator gives you one more day.
Stand on the neck of Fearful Mind.

Do not wait to open your heart.
Let yourself go into the Mystery.
Sometimes the threads have no weave.
The price of not loving yourself is high.

—Jim Cohn

Change, move, dead clock, that this fresh day
May break with dazzling light to these sick eyes.
Burn, glare, old sun, so long unseen,
That time may find its sound again, and cleanse
Whatever it is that a wound remembers
After the healing ends.

—Weldon Kees

The herbs of the field and
the symbols of land
bring healing and bless
as they come through my hand.

I welcome the fruits,
I welcome new birth,
as old wounds are healed
in the joy
of the earth.

—Nancy Rose Meeker

When the wind blows
　　that is my medicine
When it rains
　　that is my medicine
When it hails
　　that is my medicine
When it becomes clear after a storm
　　that is my medicine

—Anonymous

273

I am not a mechanism, an assembly of various sections.
And it is not because the mechanism is working wrongly,
　　that I am ill.
I am ill because of wounds to the soul,
　　to the deep emotional self
and the wounds to the soul take a long, long time,
　　only time can help
and patience, and a certain difficult repentance,
long, difficult repentance, realisation of life's mistake,
and the
　　freeing oneself
from the endless repetition of the mistake

which mankind at large has chosen to sanctify.

—D. H. Lawrence

Your pain is the breaking of the shell
　　that encloses your understanding.
Even as the stone of the fruit must break,
　　that its heart may stand in the sun,
　　so must you know pain.
And could you keep your heart in wonder
　　at the daily miracles of your life,
　　your pain would not seem less wondrous than your joy;
And you would accept the seasons of your heart,
　　even as you have always accepted the seasons
　　that pass over your fields.
And you would watch with serenity
　　through the winters of your grief.

　　　　　　　　　　　　　　　—Kahlil Gibran

Don't look back,
battered child.
Time then hurt you.
Let time heal you.
Don't look back.

Don't look back,
beaten child.
They knew not what
they did except what
was done unto them.
Don't look back.

Don't look back,
abandoned child,
abused, neglected child.
  Denial is salt in your wounds.
  Dwelling is repeating
  the deliberate disappearance
  of your soul.
  Don't perpetuate this harm.

    Break the cycle,

        wait—

            stop it here.

  Speak out the paralyzing secret
  and begin to come back to yourself.
  Cry it out to compassionate ears
  and be held in the hearts of your witnesses.

  The truth shall make you free
  but first it will shatter you.
  What was broken can be mended,
  what was lost, restored.
  Find yourself, then,
  pure and whole, a child of God.
  Look back long enough to let go.
                    —Alla Renée Bozarth

I need somebody
to touch me
in a healing way

Somebody

Somebody

to touch me—
with love

somebody
who can hold
this depth of pain

hold me
crying tears
for every woman
whose
being a woman
has ever
made her cry

Unshed grief
running out slowly
in a river
of cleansing salt

—Akasha Hull

In the house made of dawn.
In the story made of dawn.
On the trail of dawn.
O, Talking God!
His feet, my feet, restore
His limbs, my limbs, restore.
His body, my body, restore.
His mind, my mind, restore.
His voice, my voice, restore.
His plumes, my plumes, restore.
With beauty before him, with beauty before me.
With beauty behind him, with beauty behind me.
With beauty above him, with beauty above me.
With beauty below him, with beauty below me.
With beauty around him, with beauty around me.
With pollen beautiful in his voice, with pollen beautiful
       in my voice.
It is finished in beauty.
It is finished in beauty.
In the house of evening light.
From the story made of evening light.
On the trail of evening light.

                  —Navajo prayer

A small wave for your form
  A small wave for your voice
    A small wave for your speech
A small wave for your means
  A small wave for your generosity
    A small wave for your appetite
A small wave for your wealth
  A small wave for your life
    A small wave for your health.
Nine waves of grace upon you.
Waves of the Giver of Health.

—Mhairi nic Neill

God our Mother,
Living Water,
River of Mercy,
Source of Life,
in whom we live
and move
and have our being,
who quenches our thirst,
refreshes our weariness,
bathes
and washes
and cleanses
our wounds,
be for us always
a fountain of life,
and for all the world
a river of hope
springing up in the midst
of the deserts of despair.
Honor and blessing,
glory and praise
to You forever.

Amen.

—Medical Mission Sisters

279

Beloved Lord, Almighty God!
Through the rays of the sun,
Through the waves of the air,
Through the All-pervading Life in space,
Purify and revivify me, and, I pray.
Heal my body, heart, and soul.
> Amen.

> —Hazrat Inayat Khan

Friend, you lie quiet,
watching the dawn light color your heart,
dreaming of healing for your hurt body
laying there unanswerable to your will.
You breathe deep and your breath has two sides:
    inside and outside. You are on both, being breathed.
The future approaches. You will heal or
you will go back to being God.
Which will you do?

Oh by all that is beautiful—
May it be that you live!
May your body heal happy and whole!
May energy fill and delight you!
May we join the dance your presence gives!
May you live!

And if you die?
Oh dear self, by all that is beautiful,
Know you are Safe! Everything is All Right
Forever and Ever and Ever!
The most wonderful, exquisite, familiar
Truth is what is True, and welcomes you.
It will be very easy.

You lie quiet now, praying.
A great healing is coming
and you want to be ready.
The colors of your heart blend
with the light of the morning.
You are blessed.

—Elias Amidon

Midlife

My fiftieth year had come and gone,
I sat, a solitary man,
In a crowded London shop,
An open book and empty cup
On the marble table-top.

While on the shop and street I gazed
My body of a sudden blazed;
And twenty minutes more or less
It seemed, so great my happiness,
That I was blessed and could bless.
                            —William Butler Yeats

Brushing out my daughter's dark
silken hair before the mirror
I see the grey gleaming on my head,
the silver-haired servant behind her. Why is it
just as we begin to go
they begin to arrive, the fold in my neck
clarifying as the fine bones of her
hips sharpen? As my skin shows
its dry pitting, she opens like a small
pale flower on the tip of a cactus;
as my last chances to bear a child
are falling through my body, the duds among them,
her purse full of eggs, round and
firm as hard-boiled yolks, is about
to snap its clasp. I brush her tangled
fragrant hair at bedtime. It's an old
story—the oldest we have on our planet—
the story of replacement.

—Sharon Olds

Mother, I need you. Though a woman grown,
Mine own self's arbiter, mine own law,
My need for you is deeper than I've known,
And far more urgent than it was before.
Into your tender arms I'd love to creep,
Pour out my woes, and cry myself to sleep.

But even were you here, this could not be,
Convention kills the sobbing child in me,
Since soft white luster crowned your smooth fair brow,
'Tis I, the child, turns Mother to you now.
Then whilst my firm hand smooths your long white hair,
And my young lips press from your eyes the tears,
Whilst my strong arms are round you, resting there in my embrace
I loose the weight of years.
And when you smile, confiding tilt your head,
To gaze into my eyes, I'm comforted.
　　　　　—Gladys May Casely-Hayford ("Aquah Laluah")

To you, my father, I reach, almost touching,
your eight decades of moments falling away
like huge snowflakes in the lamplight,
watching how you wait with such sad curiosity
for the end of the storm—

and to you, my teenage son, I reach, almost touching,
as in ignorance and faith you assume
the debts of our race
and I am helpless to save you.

How intimate, how distant, we three men—
walking away from each other on the same ground,
good-hearted, mortal, and
how dear we are, to walk in this world
so innocent, so weathered, so amazed.

We are the generations of men
hoping to do our best
in a world we didn't ask for.
May a way be prepared for us,
may our gestures be pure,
may we bless the future
with the continuity of our love.

—Elias Amidon

My brother lives too far away
For me to see him when I would;
Which is now; is every day;
Is always, always; so I say
When I remember our boyhood.

So close together, long ago,
And he the one that knew me best;
He the one that loved me so,
Himself was nothing; this I know
Too late for my own love to rest.

It runs to tell him I have learned
At last the secret: he was I.
And still he is, though time has turned
Us back to back, and age has burned
This difference in us till we die.

—Mark Van Doren

289

Is it morning,
really morning,
or is it just
another day?
A new beginning
or just a continuing
yesterday?
How I wish for morning:
a light soft
and bleaching a night's pain.
A new beginning,
a new day.
But I fear morning's no longer with me.
Beginnings rarely seek me out—
I am too much with middles.

                    —Rabbi Rami M. Shapiro

Why are you waiting
   to begin your life?
Do you think the world must
   care
   and come soliciting?
Listen to the knocking
   at the door of your own
   heart
It is only faint because
   you have not answered
You have fooled yourself
   with preparations
Time left laughing
   while you considered possibilities
Wake up
   you have slept long enough
Wake up
   tomorrow may be too late

When you finally dare open
   the door
   your life will begin arriving
Cautiously at first
   unbelieving that the gate
So long locked against the tide
   has finally been opened
Then with swells
   of neglected dreams
Then with waves of joyful
   revelation
   the sea will follow
You will be swept by the full
   and magnificent tides
   of your own longing
That no one else can give you
   That no one else can claim
         —Judith Gass

Literally thin-skinned, I suppose, my face
catches the wind off the snow line and flushes
with a flush that will never wholly settle. Well:
that was a metropolitan vanity,
wanting to look young forever, to pass.

I was never a pre-Raphaelite beauty,
nor anything but pretty enough to satisfy
men who need to be seen with passable women.
But now that I am in love with a place
that doesn't care how I look, or if I'm happy,

happy is how I look, and that's all.
My hair will turn grey in any case,
my nails chip and flake, my waist thicken,
and the years work all their usual changes.
If my face is to be weather-beaten as well

that's little enough lost, a fair bargain
for a year among lakes and fells, when simply
to look out of my window at the high pass
makes me indifferent to mirrors and to what
my soul may wear over its new complexion.
                                    —Fleur Adcock

She has been with me all day,
   yet now it is as if i see her
      for the first time.

Green succulent leaves
   full of the life juice
      that feeds this stalk taller than i.
The stout stem comes thrusting
   out of her with perseverance
      to produce the flower
that is the essence of her life.

She has been speaking to me all day.
   yet now i finally hear her story.

Beside her are the remains of her past life.
   the same plant, but
      leaves are brown and baked,
      stalk parched and leaning
      seed pods dry and empty.
Agave blooms just once.

And i pray that i too
   may bloom
      before i die.

                              —Mavis Muller

After a while you learn
The subtle difference
Between holding a hand
And chaining a soul.

And you learn
That love doesn't mean leaning
And company doesn't mean security.
And you begin to learn
That kisses aren't compromises
And presents aren't promises.
And you begin to accept your defeats
With your head up and your eyes ahead
With the grace of a woman or man
Not the grief of a child.
And you learn to build all your loads on today
Because tomorrow's ground is too uncertain for plans
And futures have a way of falling down in midflight.
After a while you learn
That even sunshine burns if you ask too much.
So you plant your own garden
And decorate your own soul
Instead of waiting for someone to buy you flowers.
And you learn
That you really can endure
That you really are strong
And you really do have worth.
And you learn.

And you learn.
With every failure you learn.

—Anonymous

Nothing seems to get any better
I have given up waiting for more
Once we had youth on our side
full of promise
Now we are what we are
and struggle with one aging mind
to climb the wall
we no longer believe is there

—Dan Gerber

If you imagine
if you imagine
little sweetie little sweetie
if you imagine
this will this will this
will last forever
this season of
this season of
season of love
you're fooling yourself
little sweetie little sweetie
you're fooling yourself

If you think little one
if you think ah ah
that that rosy complexion
that waspy waist
those lovely muscles
the enamel nails
nymph thigh
and your light foot
if you think little one
that will that will that
will last forever
you're fooling yourself
little sweetie little sweetie
you're fooling yourself

The lovely days disappear
the lovely holidays
suns and planets
go round in a circle
but you my little one
you go straight
toward you know not what
very slowly draw near
the sudden wrinkle
the weighty fat
the triple chin
the flabby muscle
come gather gather
the roses the roses
roses of life
and may their petals
be a calm sea
of happinesses
come gather gather
if you don't do it
you're fooling yourself
little sweetie little sweetie
you're fooling yourself
　　　—Raymond Queneau
　　　　　(translated by
　　　　Michael Benedikt)

Mountains loom upon the path we take;
Yonder peak now rises sharp and clear;
Behold! It stands with its head uplifted,
Thither go we, since our way lies there.

Mountains loom upon the path we take;
Yonder peak now rises sharp and clear;
Behold! We climb, drawing near its summit;
Steeper grows the way and slow our steps.

Mountains loom upon the path we take;
Yonder peak that rises sharp and clear,
Behold us now on its head uplifted;
Planting there our feet, we stand secure.

Mountains loom upon the path we take;
Yonder peak that rose sharp and clear:
Behold us now on its head uplifted;
Resting there at last, we sing our song.
                              —Pawnee song

297

When I was a youngster
   I wanted to go out running
   among the mountain peaks
And when, between two summits
   a gap appeared,
   why not leap
   across the chasm?
Led by the angel's hand,
   all my life long
   this is what happened,
   this, exactly.

                —Dom Helder Camara

I am of the nature to grow old.
There is no way to escape growing old.

I am of the nature to have ill-health.
There is no way to escape having ill-health.

I am of the nature to die.
There is no way to escape death.

All that is dear to me and everyone I love
are of the nature to change.
There is no way to escape being separated from them.

My actions are my only true belongings.
I cannot escape the consequences of my actions.
My actions are the ground on which I stand.

—The Buddha

Friend, hope for the Guest while you are alive.
Jump into experience while you are alive! . . .
  What you call "salvation" belongs to the time before death.

If you don't break your ropes while you are alive,
do you think
ghosts will do it after?

The idea that the soul will join with the ecstatic
just because the body is rotten—
that is all fantasy.
What is found now is found then.
If you find nothing now,
you will simply end up with an apartment in the City
    of Death.
If you make love with the divine now, in the next life
    you will have the face of satisfied desire . . .
                    —Kabir (version by Robert Bly)

Ten thousand flowers in spring,
the moon in autumn,
a cool breeze in summer,
snow in winter.
If your mind isn't clouded by
unnecessary things,
this is the best season of your life.

—Wu-Men

Birth is a beginning and Death a destination;
From childhood to maturity and youth to age,
From innocence to awareness and ignorance to knowing.
From foolishness to discretion and then, perhaps to wisdom.
From weakness to strength or strength to weakness, and back again.
From health to sickness and back, we pray, to health again.
From offense to forgiveness, from loneliness to love.
From joy to gratitude, from pain to compassion.
From grief to understanding, from fear to faith.
From defeat to defeat
Until looking backward or ahead, we see that
Victory lies not at some high place along the way,
But in having made the Journey, stage by stage.

—Yom Kippur prayer

The longer we are together
the larger death grows around us.
How many we know by now
who are dead! We, who were young,
now count the cost of having been.
And yet as we know the dead
we grow familiar with the world.
We, who were young and loved each other
ignorantly, now come to know
each other in love, married
by what we have done, as much
as by what we intend. Our hair
turns white with our ripening
as though to fly away in some
coming wind, bearing the seed
of what we know. It was bitter to learn
that we come to death as we come
to love, bitter to face
the just and solving welcome
that death prepares. But that is bitter
only to the ignorant, who pray
it will not happen. Having come
the bitter way to better prayer, we have
the sweetness of ripening. How sweet
to know you by the signs of this world!
                              —Wendell Berry

Growing Older

Let others speak
of harps and
heavenly choirs
I've made my decision
to remain here
with the Earth

if the old grey poet
felt he could turn and
live with the animals
why should I be too good
to stay and die with them

and the great road of the Milky Way,
that Sky Trail my Abenaki ancestors
strode to the last Happy home
does not answer my dreams

I do not believe
we go up to the sky
unless it is
to fall again
with the rain

—Joseph Bruchac

Eternal wisdom, source of our being,
and center of all our longing,
in you our sister has lived to a strong age:
a woman of dignity and wit,
in loving insight now a blessed crone.
May the phase into which she has entered
bear the marks of your spirit.
May she ever be borne up
by the fierce and tender love of friends
and by you, most intimate friend;
and clothed in your light,
grow in grace as she advances in years;
for your love's sake. Amen

—Gail A. Ricciuti

Beautiful are the youth
whose rich emotions flash and burn,
whose lithe bodies filled with energy and grace
sway in their happy dance of life;
and beautiful likewise are the mature
who have learned compassion and patience, charity and wisdom,
    though they
be rarer far than beautiful youth.

But most beautiful and most rare is a gracious old age
which has drawn from life the skill to take its varied strands: the
    harsh
advance of age, the pang of grief,
the passing of dear friends, the loss of strength,
and with fresh insight weave them
into a rich and gracious pattern all its own.
This is the greatest skill of all,
to take the bitter with the sweet and make it beautiful,
to take the whole of life in all its moods,
its strengths and weaknesses,
and of the whole make one great and celestial harmony.
                                        —Robert Terry Weston

Comes the dust falling in the air
comes in the afternoon the sunbeam
comes through the sound of friends
comes the shadow through the door
comes the unturned page
comes the name
comes the footstep
comes to each wall the portrait
comes the white hair

comes with the flowers opening
comes as the hands touch and stay
comes with late fortune and late seed
comes with the whole of music
comes with the light on the mountains
comes at the hours of clouds
comes the white hair

comes the sudden widening of the river
comes as the birds disappear in the air
comes while we talk together
comes as we listen to each other
comes as we are lying together
comes while we sleep
comes the white hair

—W. S. Merwin

Our old women gods, we ask you!
Our old women gods, we ask you!
Then give us long life together,
May we live until our frosted hair
Is white; may we live till then
This life that now we know!

—Tewa prayer

I invoke the seven daughters of Ocean
who weave the threads of the sons of age.
Three deaths be taken from me,
three life-times be given me,
seven waves of surety be granted me.
No illusions disturb my journey,
in brilliant breastplate without hurt.
My honour shall not be bound by oblivion.
Welcome age! death shall not corrupt the old.

I invoke the Silver One, undying and deathless,
may my life be enduring as white-bronze!
May my rights be upheld!
May my strength be increased!
May my grave not be dug!
May death not visit me!
May my journey be fulfilled!
I shall not be devoured by the headless adder,
nor by the hard green tick,
nor by the headless beetle.
I shall not be injured by a bevy of women
nor a gang of armed men.
May the King of the Universe stretch time for me!

—Celtic prayer

In my young days I never
Tasted sorrow. I wanted
To become a famous poet.
I wanted to get ahead
So I pretended to be sad.
Now I am old and have known
The depths of every sorrow,
And I am content to loaf
And enjoy the clear Autumn.

—Hsin Ch'i Chi

311

I'm not ashamed at my age to stick a flower in my hair.
The flower is the embarrassed one, topping an old man's head.
People laugh as I go home drunk, leaning on friends—
ten miles of elegant blinds raised halfway for watching.

—Su Tung-p'o

Methought, I had no desire of living longer;
Yet, why should I not long to see another year,
Again this pure moonlight of restful autumn?

My gaze is caught by the butterflies
Playing among flowers that bloom on the hedge;
Do I envy them?—yes, perhaps—Am I envying
These little creatures, friends of the flowers?

312

Charmed by the flowers, I seem to feel a love for them.
How can this passion still possess my soul,
When, methought, I had utterly renounced the world!

—Saigyo

For eighty years I've talked of east and west:
What nonsense. What's long/short? big/small?
There's no need of the gray old man, I'm one
With all of you, in everything. Once through
The emptiness of all, who's coming? Who's going?

—Kiyo

Friend, please tell me what I can do about this
world
I hold to, and keep spinning out!

I gave up sewn clothes, and wore a robe,
but noticed one day the cloth was well woven.

So I bought some burlap, but I still
throw it elegantly over my left shoulder.

I pulled back my sexual longings,
and now discover that I'm angry a lot.

I gave up rage, and now I notice
that I am greedy all day.

I worked hard at dissolving the greed,
and now I am proud of myself.

When the mind wants to break its link with the world
it still holds on to one thing.

—Kabir

314

There are few of us now, soon
There will be none. We were comrades
Together, we believed we
Would see with our own eyes the new
World where man was no longer
Wolf to man, but men and women
Were all brothers and lovers
Together. We will not see it.
We will not see it, none of us.
It is farther off than we thought.
In our young days we believed
That as we grew old and fell
Out of rank, new recruits, young
And with the wisdom of youth,
Would take our places and they
Surely would grow old in the
Golden Age. They have not come.
They will not come. There are not
Many of us left. Once we
Marched in closed ranks, today each
Of us fights off the enemy,
A lonely isolated guerrilla.
All this has happened before,
Many times. It does not matter.
We were comrades together.
Life was good for us. It is
Good to be brave—nothing is
Better. Food tastes better. Wine
Is more brilliant. Girls are more

Beautiful. The sky is bluer
For the brave—for the brave and
Happy comrades and for the
Lonely brave retreating warriors.
You had a good life. Even all
Its sorrows and defeats and
Disillusionments were good,
Met with courage and a gay heart.
You are gone and we are that
Much more alone. We are one fewer,
Soon we shall be none. We know now
We have failed for a long time.
And we do not care. We few will
Remember as long as we can,
Our children may remember,
Some day the world will remember.
Then they will say, "They lived in
The days of the good comrades.
It must have been wonderful
To have been alive then, though it
Is very beautiful now."
We will be remembered, all
Of us, always, by all men,
In the good days now so far away.
If the good days never come,
We will not know. We will not care.
Our lives were the best. We were the
Happiest men alive in our day.

—Kenneth Rexroth

315

Initiations: Growing Older

In the quiet before cockcrow when the cricket's
Mandolin falters, when the light of the past
Falling from the high stars yet haunts the earth
And the east quickens, I think of those I love—
Dear men and women no longer with us.

And not in grief or regret merely but rather
With a love that is almost joy I think of them,
Of whom I am part, as they of me, and through whom
I am made more wholly one with the pain and the glory,
The heartbreak at the heart of things.

I have learned it from them at last, who am now grown old
A happy man, that the nature of things is tragic
And meaningful beyond words, that to have lived
Even if once only, once and no more,
Will have been—oh, how truly—worth it.

The years go by: March flows into April,
The sycamore's delicate tracery puts on
Its tender green; April is August soon;
Autumn, and the raving of insect choirs,
The thud of apples in moonlit orchards;

Till winter brings the slant, windy light again
On shining Manhattan, her towering stone and glass;
And age deepens—oh, much is taken, but one
Dearer than all remains, and life is sweet
Still, to the now enlightened spirit . . .

Truly, to me they now may come no more,
But I to them in reverie and remembrance
Still may return, in me they still live on;
In me they shall have their being, till we together
Darken in the great memory.

Dear eyes of delight, dear youthful tresses, foreheads
Furrowed with age, dear hands of love and care—
Lying awake at dawn, I remember them,
With a love that is almost joy I remember them:
Lost, and all mine, all mine, forever.
                                    —John Hall Wheelock

317

When I remember all
    The friends so linked together
I've seen around me fall,
    Like leaves in wintry weather,
        I feel like one
        Who treads alone
Some banquet-hall deserted,
        Whose lights are fled,
        Whose garlands are dead,
    And all but him departed!
Thus in the stilly night,
    Ere Slumber's chain has bound me,
Sad memory brings the light
    Of other days around me.

—Thomas Moore

This will happen
Oh god we say just give
me a few more
breaths
and don't let it be
terrible
let it be soft
perhaps in someone's
arms, perhaps tasting
chocolate
perhaps
laughing or asking
Is it over already?
or saying *not yet. Not*
yet the sky
has at this moment turned
another shade of blue,
and see there a child
still plays
in the fresh snow.

—Susan Griffin

1

When I was green, everyone loved me. Bees
crooned my sweetness; butterflies made me their own.
But then something called time began to drag me
away and I became curled up and brittle and brown.

2

These lines you read are what an oak leaf wrote,
following a storm that dragged it over the snow—
complaining and kicking. "I don't want to forsake
my tree. Help! Where did my sisters go?"

3

When spring comes, a whole new cast will have the stage
and I will huddle where winter threw me away,
but wherever I am the soil will be bitter because
I remember how lonely it was when I tried to stay.

4

This farewell comes from a forgiving leaf
that skipped with the others and then found a lucky storm
that brought me here. Listen—hold on as long
as you can, then thrust forth: make truth your home.

—Willliam Stafford

People expect old men to die,
They do not really mourn old men.
Old men are different. People look
At them with eyes that wonder when . . .
People watch with unshocked eyes;
But the old men know when an old man dies.

—Ogden Nash

The old men
    now are so few
    that they are not worth counting.
I myself am
    the last living,
    therefore
    a hard time
    I am having.

—Teton Sioux song

Initiations: Growing Older

All that I serve will die, my delights,
the flesh kindled from my flesh, garden and field,
the silent lilies standing in the woods,
the woods, the hill, the whole earth, all
will burn in man's evil, or dwindle
in its own age. Let the world bring on me
the sleep of darkness without stars, so I may know
my little light taken from me into the seed
of the beginning and the end, so I may bow
to mystery, and take my stand on the earth
like a tree in a field, passing without haste
or regret toward what will be, my life
a patient willing descent into the grass.

—Wendell Berry

I am luminous with age
In my lap I hold the valley.
I see on the horizon what has been taken
What is gone lies prone fleshless.
In my breast I hold the middle valley
The corn kernels cry to me in the fields
    Take us home.
Like corn I cry in the last sunset
Gleam like plums.
    My bones shine in fever
Smoked with the fires of age.
Herbal, I contain the final juice,
Shadow, I crouch in the ash
    never breaking to fire.
Winter iron bough
    unseen my buds,
Hanging close I live in the beloved bone
Speaking in the marrow
    alive in green memory.

The light was brighter then.
Now spiders creep at my eyes' edge.
I peek between my fingers
    at my fathers' dust.
The old stones have been taken away
    there is no path.

Initiations: Growing Older

The fathering fields are gone.
The wind is stronger than it used to be.
My stone feet far below me grip the dust.
I run and crouch in corners with thin dogs.
I tie myself to the children like a kite.
I fall and burst beneath the sacred human tree.
Release my seed and let me fall.
Toward the shadow of the great earth
    let me fall.

       —Meridel LeSueur

From too much love of living,
 From hope and fear set free,
We thank with brief thanksgiving   ·
 Whatever gods may be
That no life lives forever;
That dead men rise up never;
That even the weariest river
 Winds somewhere safe to sea.

     —Algernon Charles Swinburne

Death

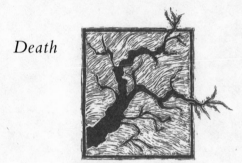

Not for me steel coffins
Nor even a pinewood box.
Lay me out in the wilderness
And let me return to Earth.

Tear my flesh, coyote
And I will run with you
over the plains.
Take my eyes, eagle
And I will soar with you
In the mountains.
Pick my bones clean, little beetles
And I will flow back
Into the lifestream
To think like a mountain
And sing like a river.

—Mary de La Valette

327

My child, you have toiled through life and come to the end of suffering: and now our lord has obliged you.

Now you have gone, gone to whatever kind of place it may be, the place where all are shorn, the place we all go to, the place of no lights and no windows, never again to return, to come back. You will think no more of what lies here, of what lies behind you.

At the end of many days you went away and left your children, your grandchildren; you left them orphaned, you left them living. You will think no more of what may become of them.

We will go and join you, we will go be with you at the end of many days.

—Aztec prayer

Deep wet moss and cool blue shadows
　　Beneath a bending fir,
And the purple solitude of mountains,
　　When only the dark owls stir—
Oh, there will come a day, a twilight,
　　When I shall sink to rest
In deep wet moss and cool blue shadows
　　Upon a mountain's breast,
And yield a body torn with passions,
　　And bruised with earthly scars,
To the cool oblivion of evening,
　　Of solitude and stars.

　　　　　　　　　　—Lew Sarett

329

You shall ask
What good are dead leaves
And I will tell you
They nourish the sore earth.
You shall ask
What reason is there for winter
And I will tell you
To bring about new leaves.
You shall ask
Why are the leaves so green
And I will tell you
Because they are rich with life
You shall ask
Why must summer end
And I will tell you
So that the leaves can die.

—Nancy Wood

Out of life comes death,
and out of death, life,
Out of the young, the old,
and out of the old, the young,
Out of waking, sleep,
and out of sleep, waking,
The stream of creation and dissolution
never stops.

—Heraclitus

If you would indeed behold the spirit
    of death, open your heart wide
    unto the body of life.
For life and death are one, even as the
    river and the sea are one.

—Kahlil Gibran

Earth the mighty and the ether of Zeus,
He is the begetter of men and gods;
And she, when she has caught the rain's moist drops,
Gives birth to mortals,
Gives birth to pasture and the beasts after their kinds.
Whence not unjustly
She is deemed mother of all things.
But that which has been born of earth
To earth returns;
And that which has sprouted from ethereal seed
To heaven's vault goes back.
So nothing dies of all that into being comes,
But each from each is parted
And so takes another form.

—Euripides

Birth.
Impossible to imagine
not knowing how to expect.

Childbirth.
Impossible to imagine
years of the tall son.

Death,
impossible to imagine,
exactly, exactly.

—Anne Stevenson

———

In the great night my heart will go out;
Toward me the darkness comes rustling.
In the great night my heart will go out.

—Papago prayer

She had done all she could.
There was nothing left to do.
Her children were well.
They could take care of themselves now.

No need to worry.
Final responsibilities done.
Only now to think of peace.
No more energy for the body's pain.

Leave it here. Think peace.
No one to be sad for.
That will only bring her spirit back.
Bringing the spirit back will only trouble her.

Will only hinder her making the journey.
The journey before her now.
Saying this, Don's mother let go.
Leaving her worn out body behind.

Like this, he said, the healing continues.
Like this till the end.
Until the person is in the ground
The healing must go on like this.

—Jim Cohn

I am not resigned to the shutting away of loving hearts in the
    hard ground.
So it is, and so it will be, for so it has been time out of mind:
Into the darkness they go, the wise and the lovely. Crowned
With lilies and with laurel they go; but I am not resigned.

Lovers and thinkers, into the earth with you.
Be one with the dull, the indiscriminate dust.
A fragment of what you felt, of what you knew,
A formula, a phrase remains, but the best is lost.

The answers quick and keen, the honest look, the laughter,
    the love,
They are gone. They are gone to feed the roses. Elegant and
    curled
Is the blossom. Fragrant is the blossom. I know. But I do
    not approve.
More precious was the light in your eyes than all the roses in
    the world.

Down, down into the darkness of the grave
Gently they go, the beautiful, the tender, the kind;
Quietly they go, the intelligent, the witty, the brave.
I know. But I do not approve. And I am not resigned.

        —Edna St. Vincent Millay

We cannot stay their death nor stay our death.
We can but pause and look into a glass
And see our nostrils taking in the breath
Which is the breath of life it always was.
We can touch our flesh and with a certain pride
Feel it still warm, can remember tender things
We used to say to someone who has died,
Can still be glad of present happenings,
Can still be glad that they, not we have gone
Into that shadow of eternity
Which we are not compelled to look upon
As long as there are lesser things to see.
What else is there to do, although a face
Lies quietly in its eventual place.

—Witter Bynner

Listen more often
To things than to beings;
The fire's voice is heard,
Hear the voice of water.
Hear in the wind
The bush sob:
It is the ancestors' breath.

Those who have died have never left,
They are in the brightening shadow
And in the thickening shadow;
The dead are not under the earth,
They are in the rustling tree,
They are in the groaning woods,
They are in the flowing water,
They are in the still water,
They are in the hut, they are in the crowd:
The dead are not dead.

Listen more often
To things than to beings;
The fire's voice is heard,
Hear the voice of water.
Hear in the wind
The bush sob:
It is the ancestors' breath,
The breath of dead ancestors
Who have not left,

Initiations: Death

Who are not under the earth,
Who are not dead.
Those who have died have never left,
They are in the woman's breast,
They are in the wailing child
And in the kindling firebrand.
The dead are not under the earth,
They are in the fire dying down,
They are in the moaning rock,
They are in the crying grass,
They are in the forest, they are in the home:
The dead are not dead.

—Birago Diop

Children,
when I am ash
read by the light of the fire
that consumes me
this document
whose subject is love.

I want to leave you everything: my life
divided into so many parts
there are enough to go around; the world
from this window: weather and a tree
which bequeaths
all of its leaves each year.

Today the lawyer plans
for your descendants,
telling a story
of generations
that seems to come true
even as he speaks.

My books will fill
your children's shelves,
my small enameled spoons
invade their drawers. It is
the only way I know, so far,
to haunt.

Let me be a guest at my own funeral
and at the reading of my will.
You I'll reward first
for the moments of your births,
those three brief instants
when I understood my life.

But wisdom bends as light does
around the objects it touches.
The only legacy you need was left
by accident long ago:
a secret in the genes.
The rest is small change.

—Linda Pastan

Initiations: Death

So I turn my head and look towards death now.
Feeling my way through the tunnel with the space of
emptiness and quiet.
That shimmering silence that awaits me.

I do not have a passion to remain, but a willingness to go.
My body is tired and my soul longs to fly free to the shores
of no pain.

Thoughts clutch at my gown as I make my way down the
stony corridors.
Holding me, pulling me back to concerns I am finished with.

A breath . . . A pause.
I relax, and then float on toward the opening awaiting me.
This place of peace resides so deep inside me;
It is one, huge and all encompassing.

In the quiet of my mind I find the greatest Truth, the
great Mother/Father.
This is the Hail Mary, the Rod and Staff of Comfort,
The Kingdom and the Glory.

Yea, though I walk through the valley of death,
I will fear no evil.

This is my direction now; inward to the green pastures,
to the great light of divine love, the great peace of All Knowing.
—Karen Paine-Gernee
(written shortly before her death)

When the ripe fruit falls
its sweetness distills and trickles away
into the veins of the earth.

When fulfilled people die
the essential oil of their experience enters
the veins of living space, and adds a glisten
to the atom, to the body of immortal chaos.

For space is alive
and it stirs like a swan
whose feathers glisten
silky with oil of distilled experience.
                                        —D. H. Lawrence

———

She whom we love
and lose
is no longer
where she was before.
She is now
wherever we are.
                            —St. John Chrysostom

I wasn't there when your body, signaling, woke you
When you sat, moving yourself to the edge, and stood
and knew July by its heat and wondered what time it was
and steadied yourself, sat down, and called out for my mother

When she came, her impatience visible in the air around her
because it was hot and something in a pot needed stirring
When she helped you into the slip worn thin by your patience
When she asked you which dress you wanted to wear

and when you pulled on the stockings yourself, and the garters
and stepped into your shoes and looked down and knew
and did not tell my mother you knew
When you asked her please would she comb your hair

When you sat down to the meal with my mother and father
and my father asked *would you like some of this and some of this*
When you lifted the glass and gazed through the water's prism
When you drank, swallow by swallow, all of the water

and opened the napkin but did not pick up the fork
When you folded the napkin and pushed back the plate,
pushed back the chair and stood with no help from anyone
and turned, saying nothing, and walked out of the room

When they called you   When you did not answer
When you shut the door and looked at your face in the mirror
Your face   that friend of long standing, that trustworthy sister
When you took this face in your hands to bid it goodby

and when you said to them *I want to lie down now*
When they laid you down and covered you with a sheet
and you said *Go on now, go eat* and they did
because they had worked and were hungry and this had happened
     before

When you lay back in it to let it have you
knowing what you had waited for patiently and impatiently
what you had longed and hoped for and abandoned longing and
     hoping for
and prayed for and not received was finally here

When you lay back in it to let it have you
When you heard for the last time the clink of silver
and let go the sheet, let go light on the earth
When your breath ceased to be a thing that belonged to you

I wasn't there
Forgive me
I wasn't there

—Marilyn Krysl

You waited until you were alone.
Death is a private thing.
You knew your last act
was to a different audience.

As it entered you—
oh how you must have danced!
curving toward God,
elegant and alone.

Dear one, what is it like?
Tell us! What is death?

Birth,
you say, your voice swathed in wings.
I am born in the endless beginning.
I am not. I am.

You start turning into us,
we who love you.
You weep in our sadness,
you laugh when we do,
you greet each moment fresh,
when we do.

So may your gift of loving enter our own
and be with us that way, forever.

—Elias Amidon

All goes onward and outward, nothing collapses,
And to die is different from what any one supposed,
and luckier . . .

They are alive and well somewhere,
The smallest sprout shows there is really no death,
And if there ever was, it led forward life,
and does not wait at the end to arrest it,
And ceas'd the moment life appear'd.

—Walt Whitman

When I die if you need to weep
Cry for your brother or sister
Walking the street beside you
And when you need me put your arms around anyone
And give them what you need to give me.

I want to leave you something
Something better than words or sounds.

Look for me in the people I've known or loved
And if you cannot give me away
At least let me live in your eyes and not on your mind.

You can love me most by letting hands touch hands
By letting bodies touch bodies
And by letting go of children that need to be free.

Love doesn't die, people do
So when all that's left of me is love
Give me away.

—Anonymous

I will nurse this autumn carefully,
treat its brittleness gently,
smooth its crumbling edges, its weeping afternoons.

I will rise early and go to it,
wrap it in a soft cloth
and watch its breathing.

347

I will nurture this autumn knowing
it is myself
in a pure and golden form,
and that childlike
soft words will be brought bubbling up
to be recorded in the patterns of leaves
and the low fog coming across the bay.

I will accept this death
and be content with its coming and watch
its coming
and speak of its coming in slow poems
until at last
there will be no more words,
you will hear only the sound of rain as you sleep.

—Wendy Smyer Yu

In the rising of the sun and in its going down,
  we remember them.
In the glowing of the wind and in the chill of winter,
  we remember them.
In the opening of buds and in the rebirth of spring,
  we remember them.
In the blueness of the sky and in the warmth of summer,
  we remember them.
In the rustling of leaves and in the beauty of autumn,
  we remember them.
In the beginning of the year and when it ends,
  we remember them.
When we are weary and in need of strength,
  we remember them.
When we are lost and sick at heart,
  we remember them.
When we have joys we yearn to share,
  we remember them.
So long as we live, they too shall live,
  for they are now a part of us, as
  we remember them.

—Jewish prayer

You are blessed in the Mother's eyes;
You are blessed in your children's eyes;
You are blessed in all your doings;
You are blessed in all your endings;
You are blessed and purified.
There is no pain where you are going;
There is no sadness where you are received;
There is only the happiness of going home;
There is only the bliss of having arrived.
                              —Zsuzsanna E. Budapest

Naked you came
from Earth the Mother.
Naked you return to her.
May a good wind be your road.
                              —Omaha prayer

Re-member us,
you who are living,
restore us, renew us.
Speak for our silence.
Continue our work.
Bless the breath of life.
Sing of the hidden patterns.
Weave the web of peace.

—Judith Anderson

PART SEVEN

Moments of Grace
and Illumination

Each of us is blessed with moments of grace, moments when our soul becomes clear and quiet. Our worrying stops. Our yearning and planning and waiting for fulfillment stops. There is nothing to be done since everything is already happening. Grace uncovers the mysterious essence that unites us with all beings. Through its gift, the place, the time, the sky, and ourselves are revealed in right relation. What is inside of us and what is outside of us comes together, if only for a moment.

> It was all the clods at once become
> precious; it was the barn, and the shed,
> and the windmill . . .
>   . . . for, somewhere inside, the clods are
> vaulted mansions, lines through the barn sing
> for the saints forever, the shed and windmill
> rear so glorious the sun shudders like a gong.
>   —William Stafford

In this moment and place we sense the indwelling essence of spirit and stand humbled before its mystery. We know and are known by something larger than ourselves. Grace awakens in us a natural compassion, allowing us to be kinder with ourselves and with other living beings. We open our hearts knowing the Earth to be holy.

Who can say what ignites these moments of illumination? The prayers and poems in this chapter offer us hints: Stop, they say, be wholly attentive, there is no haste. Empty yourself, bring with you "a heart that watches and receives." Yet these instructions offer no guarantee that, if followed, an experience of grace will result. They offer no foolproof guarantee. That is what makes grace amazing—it is beyond our control. It comes when we free ourselves of the illusion that we are in charge.

> As swimmers dare
> to lie face to the sky
> and water bears them,
> as hawks rest upon air
> and air sustains them,
> so would I learn to attain
> freefall, and float
> into Creator Spirit's deep embrace,
> knowing no effort earns
> that all-surrounding grace.
> —Denise Levertov

Yet "no effort" doesn't mean an abdication of attention or intention. As the Vietnamese Buddhist master Thich Nhat Hanh says very clearly, "It is not a matter of faith. / It is a matter of practice."

But how can we learn to practice with no effort? The resolution to this paradox does not rest in words, though rising up beyond the words of these prayers we can sense a quality of effortless practice in the lives of their makers. Vulnerable to the beauty of existence, they invite the world into their hearts. It speaks to them, and they listen. Grace happens.

355

Gentle me,
Holy One,
into an unclenched moment,
    a deep breath,
      a letting go
          of heavy experiences,
             of shriveling anxieties,
                of dead certainties,
that, softened by the silence,
    surrounded by the light,
      and open to the mystery,
I may be found by wholeness,
    upheld by the unfathomable,
      entranced by the simple,
        and filled with the joy
          that is you.

—Ted Loder

Enough. These few words are enough.
If not these words, this breath.
If not this breath, this sitting here.

This opening to the life
we have refused
again and again
until now.

Until now.

—David Whyte

As swimmers dare
to lie face to the sky
and water bears them,
as hawks rest upon air
and air sustains them,
so would I learn to attain
freefall, and float
into Creator Spirit's deep embrace,
knowing no effort earns
that all-surrounding grace.

—Denise Levertov

Breathing in, I know that I am breathing in.
Breathing out, I know that I am breathing out.

Breathing in, I see myself as a flower.
Breathing out, I feel flesh.

Breathing in, I see myself as a mountain.
Breathing out, I feel solid.

Breathing in, I see myself as still water.
Breathing out, I reflect things as they are.

Breathing in, I see myself as space.
Breathing out, I feel free.

       —Thich Nhat Hanh

Light the first light of the evening, as in a room
In which we rest and, for small reason, think
The world imagined is the ultimate good.

This is, therefore, the intensest rendezvous.
It is in that thought that we collect ourselves,
Out of all the indifferences, into one thing;

Within a single thing, a single shawl
Wrapped tightly round us, since we are poor,
  a warmth,
A light, a power, the miraculous influence.

Here, now, we forget each other and ourselves.
We feel the obscurity of an order, a whole,
A knowledge, that which arranged the rendezvous.

Within its vital boundary, in the mind.
We say God and the imagination are one . . .
How high that highest candle lights the dark.

Out of this same light, out of the central mind,
We make a dwelling in the evening air,
In which being there together is enough.
          —Wallace Stevens

A land not mine, still
forever memorable,
the waters of its ocean
chill and fresh.

Sand on the bottom whiter than chalk,
and the air drunk, like wine,
late sun lays bare
the rosy limbs of the pinetrees.

Sunset in the ethereal waves:
I cannot tell if the day
is ending, or the world, or if
the secret of secrets is inside me again.
                              —Anna Akhmatova

Inside this new love, die.
Your way begins on the other side.
Become the sky.
Take an axe to the prison wall.
Escape.
Walk out like someone suddenly born into color.
Do it now.
You're covered with thick cloud.
Slide out the side. Die,
and be quiet. Quietness is the surest sign
that you've died.
Your old life was a frantic running
from silence.

The speechless full moon
comes out now.

—Rumi

We look with uncertainty
Beyond the old choices for
Clear-cut answers
To a softer, more permeable aliveness
Which is every moment
At the brink of death;
For something new is being born in us
If we but let it.
We stand at a new doorway,
Awaiting that which comes . . .
Daring to be human creatures.
Vulnerable to the beauty of existence.
Learning to love.

                                        —Anne Hillman

At a certain point you say to the woods, to the sea, to the mountains, the world, Now I am ready. Now I will stop and be wholly attentive. You empty yourself and wait, listening. After a time you hear it: there is nothing there. There is nothing but those things only, those created objects, discrete, growing or holding, or swaying, being rained on or raining, held, flooding or ebbing, standing, or spread. You feel the world's word as a tension, a hum, a single chorused note everywhere the same. This is it: this hum is the silence . . .

The silence is all there is. It is the alpha and the omega. It is God's brooding over the face of the waters; it is the blended note of the ten thousand things, the whine of wings. You take a step in the right direction to pray to this silence, and even to address the prayer to "World." Distinctions blur. Quit your tents. Pray without ceasing.

—Annie Dillard

It was all the clods at once become
precious; it was the barn, and the shed,
and the windmill, my hands, the crack
Arlie made in the axe handle: oh, let me stay
here humbly, forgotten, to rejoice in it all;
let the sun casually rise and set.
If I have not found the right place,
teach me; for, somewhere inside, the clods are
vaulted mansions, lines through the barn sing
for the saints forever, the shed and windmill
rear so glorious the sun shudders like a gong.

Now I know why people worship, carry around
magic emblems, wake up talking dreams
they teach to their children: the world speaks.
The world speaks everything to us.
It is our only friend.

—William Stafford

I quietly gaze into the depths of a forest
    and see nothing save beauty and peace.
Birdsong fills my ears.
A gentle breeze brushes against my cheek.
Seeing from inside the seeing,
    I drink the dark riches of the woods.

Would it be that every day
    I could see my own face so clearly in these still waters,
And meet the emptiness—which is also my very own heart—
    that is carried in the boughs of pines and in the gentle
    music of crickets.

—Cass Adams

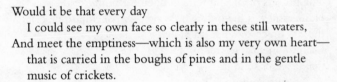

A butterfly comes and stays on a leaf—
a leaf much warmed by the sun—
and shuts his wings.
In a minute he opens them, shuts them again,
half wheels round, and by and by—
just when he chooses and not before—floats away.
The flowers open, and remain open for hours, to the sun.
Hastelessness is the only word one can make up to describe it;
there is much rest, but no haste.
Each moment is so full of life
that it seems so long
and so sufficient in itself.

—Richard Jeffries

366

Our true home is in the present moment.
To live in the present moment is a miracle.
The miracle is not to walk on water.
The miracle is to walk on the green Earth in the present moment,
to appreciate the peace and beauty that are available now.
Peace is all around us—
in the world and in nature—
and within us—
in our bodies and our spirits.
Once we learn to touch this peace,
we will be healed and transformed.
It is not a matter of faith;
it is a matter of practice.

—Thich Nhat Hanh

Happiness cannot be found through great effort and willpower,
but is already there, in relaxation and letting-go.

Don't strain yourself, there is nothing to do.
Whatever arises in the mind has no importance at all,
because it has no reality whatsoever.
Don't become attached to it.
Don't pass judgement.

Let the game happen on its own, springing up and falling back
—without changing anything—
and all will vanish and reappear, without end.

Only our searching for happiness prevents us from seeing it.
It is like a rainbow
which you run after without ever catching it.
Although it does not exist,
it has always been there and accompanies you every instant.

Don't believe in the reality of good and bad experiences;
they are like rainbows.

Waiting to grasp the ungraspable, you exhaust yourself in vain.
As soon as you relax this grasping, space is there
—open, inviting, and comfortable.

So, make us of it. All is yours already.
Don't search any further.

Don't go into the inextricable jungle looking for the elephant
who is already quietly at home.

Nothing to do,
nothing to force,
nothing to want,
—and everything happens by itself.

—Venerable Lama Gendün Rinpoche

There were times when I could not afford
to sacrifice the bloom of the present moment
to any work, whether of head or hands.
Sometimes, in a summer morning,
having taken my accustomed bath,
I sat in my sunny doorway
from sunrise till noon, rapt in a reverie,
amidst the pines and hickories and sumachs,
in undisturbed solitude and stillness,
while the birds sang around.
I grew in those seasons
like corn in the night,
and they were far better
than any work of the hands would have been.
They were not time subtracted from my life,
but so much over and above my usual allowance.

—Henry David Thoreau

The little cares that fretted me.
I lost them yesterday
Among the fields above the sea.
Among the winds at play;
Among the lowing of the herds,
The rustling of the trees,
Among the singing of the birds,
The humming of the bees.

The foolish fears of what may happen,
I cast them all away
Among the clover-scented grass,
Among the new-mown hay;
Among the husking of the corn
Where drowsy poppies nod,
Where ill thoughts die and good are born,
Out in the fields with God.

     —Elizabeth Barrett Browning

Last night, as I was sleeping,
I dreamt—marvelous error!—
that a spring was breaking
out in my heart.
I said: Along which secret aqueduct,
Oh water, are you coming to me,
water of a new life
that I have never drunk?

Last night, as I was sleeping,
I dreamt—marvelous error!—
that I had a beehive
here inside my heart.
And the golden bees
were making white combs
and sweet honey
from my old failures.

Last night, as I was sleeping,
I dreamt—marvelous error!—
that a fiery sun was giving
light inside my heart.
It was fiery because I felt
warmth as from a hearth
and sun because it gave light
and brought tears to my eyes.

Last night, as I slept,
I dreamt—marvelous error!—
that it was God I had
here inside my heart.

—Antonio Machado

Ah, not to be cut off,
not through the slightest partition
shut out from the law of the stars.
The inner—what is it?
if not intensified sky,
hurled through with birds and deep
with the winds of homecoming.

—Rainer Maria Rilke

I like to live in the sound of water,
in the feel of the mountain air. A sharp
reminder hits me: this world still is alive;
it stretches out there shivering toward its own
creation, and I'm part of it. Even my breathing
enters into this elaborate give-and-take,
this bowing to sun and moon, day or night,
winter, summer, storm, still—this tranquil
chaos that seems to be going somewhere.
This wilderness with a great peacefulness in it.
This motionless turmoil, this everything dance.
                                    —William Stafford

Enough of science and art,
Close up these barren leaves;
Come forth, and bring with you a heart
That watches and receives.
                        —William Wordsworth

Does one really have to fret
About enlightenment?
No matter what road I travel,
I'm going home.

                        —Shinsho

Moments of Grace and Illumination

This is It
and I am It
and You are It
and so is
That
and He is It
and She is It
and It is It
and That is That.

O It is This
and It is Thus
and It is Them
and It is Us
and It is Now
and here It is
and here We are
so This is It.

—James Broughton

PART EIGHT

Earth Praises

O VER the course of our life we continually offer up prayers—
whether we call them that or not—prayers spontaneous and
urgent, prayers written and thoughtful, prayers of petition and of
peace. These are our *life prayers*. They express our deepest intentions, values, and wishes. Their scope and beauty are in evidence
throughout the pages of this book. Now in this final chapter we
turn to what has been called the very heart of prayer: praise and
gratefulness.

In a world that puts great value on material acquisitions, progress, and power, why praise the Earth? Why give thanks? It has been
said that praise and gratefulness complete creation. When our
hearts receive the beauty of the world, then the circle of gifting is
complete, and we become fully present to life.

> O Thou, the sustainer of our bodies, hearts, and souls,
> Bless all that we receive in thankfulness.
>
> —Hazrat Inayat Khan

This simple grace reminds us that the food we eat and the life
we are given become a blessing when we are thankful. Our gratitude transforms the world from objects and mundane experiences

to blessings—it sacralizes the world. Our joy in the beauty of the Earth is an essential part of that beauty.

Prayers of gratitude and praise are a gateway through which this beauty enters our lives. They give us a common vision of the wondrous blue-green planet that is our home. We are born of the Earth. The Earth is our origin, our nourishment, our support, and the container of all spiritual revelation. Our spirituality itself has arisen from the spirituality of the Earth: We are totally implicated in one another's presence and identities.

Touched by gratitude we realize that we *belong* here, and in our mutual dependence we are freed to love this world wholeheartedly. It may be that the greatest gift we humans can give the rest of creation is our love and our heartfelt appreciation. Our love is as essential a part of life's give-and-take as the cycles of water and oxygen or any other nourishment flowing through the biosphere. And for millennia prayers and songs of praise have been offered up to celebrate the miracle of existence:

> . . . I know nothing else but miracles . . .
> To me every hour of the light and dark is a miracle,
> Every cubic inch of space is a miracle,
> Every square yard of the surface of the earth is spread with miracles,
> Every foot of the interior swarms with miracles.
> —Walt Whitman

May our voices join in this lineage of prayer celebrating the ordinary miracles of our lives!

The mother of us all,
the oldest of all,
hard,
    splendid as rock

Whatever there is that is of the land
        it is she
            who nourishes it,
        it is the Earth
                that I sing
Whoever you are,
howsoever you come
        across her sacred ground
    you of the sea,
    you that fly,
it is she
who nourishes you
she,
    out of her treasures
                Beautiful children
                beautiful harvests
                    are achieved from you
                The giving of life itself,
                the taking of it back
                    —The Homeric Hymns
                (translated by Charles Boer)

379

I am the beauty of the green earth
And the white moon among the stars
And the mystery of the waters
And the desire of human hearts.

Call unto your soul: Arise and come unto me
For I am the soul of nature who gives
Life to the universe.
From me all things proceed
And unto me all things must return.

—Doreen Valiente

The earth is all that lasts.
The earth is what I speak to when
I do not understand my life
Nor why I am not heard.
The earth answers me with the same song
That it sang for my fathers when
Their tears covered up the sun.
The earth sings a song of gladness.
The earth sings a song of praise.
The earth rises up and laughs at me
Each time that I forget
How spring begins with winter
And death begins with birth.

—Nancy Wood

381

Please, dear mother Earth,
Help me to stand firm on my own two feet
Drawing on the solid earth below me
Help me to know the constancy of your strength
the power that is you, oh dear mother earth
    Help me to walk with the blood of rivers in my veins
and the dark crumbling soil of earth in my flesh
Let my muscles be strong as the tree trunks
that rise up out of your belly
To dance in the sky
and sing praises to the life all around
Beating, pulsing, rich and full
with your sweet sure energy.
Oh dear mother earth,
Live in this body today.
Sing loudly in every breath I take
Stretch wildly and flow freely
with all the directions I move
and come home with me,
come home to my belly
live deep in my soul
oh mother earth, SING!

—Stephanie Kaza

For the earth forever turning;
For the skies, for every sea;
To the Lord we sing returning
Home to our blue green hills of earth.

For the mountains, hills and pastures
In their silent majesty;
For all life, for all of Nature
Sing we our joyful praise to Thee.

For the sun, for rain and thunder;
For the land that makes us free;
For the start, for all the heavens,
Sing we our joyful praise to Thee.

For the earth forever turning;
For the skies, for every sea;
To our Lord we sing returning
Home to our blue green hills of earth.

—Kim Oler

Sing to Life a new song!
Sing to Life, all Creation!
    Sing of compassion and
    temper your deeds with kindness.
Sing to all the world and
tell of the miracles that sustain us daily.
    Yet Wonder is greater than praise,
    no words can capture its Essence.
All words are idols, all ideas snares—
Truth is beyond opinion,
Reality lies beyond thought's last horizon.
    Splendor and majesty leave us speechless.
    Strength and beauty are touched not talked.
Let your worship be acts of beauty and holiness;
Let all the world stand together in awe.
    Declare among the nations: "All is God!
    Maintain the world with justice!"
The heavens rejoice and the earth is glad;
the seas roar their praise.
    The fields exult; the forests sing.
    For all the world is rooted in righteousness.
                        —Rabbi Rami M. Shapiro

The world is charged with the grandeur of God.
 It will flame out, like shining from shook foil;
 It gathers to a greatness, like the ooze of oil
Crushed. Why do men then now not reck his rod?
Generations have trod, have trod, have trod;
 And all is seared with trade; bleared, smeared with toil;
 And wears man's smudge and shares man's smell: the soil
Is bare now, nor can foot feel, being shod.

And for all this, nature is never spent;
 There lives the dearest freshness deep down things;
And though the last lights off the black West went
 Oh, morning, at the brown brink eastward, springs—
Because the Holy Ghost over the bent
 World broods with warm breast and with ah! bright
  wings.

—Gerald Manley Hopkins

How wonderful, O Lord,
are the works of your hands!
The heavens declare Your glory,
the arch of sky displays Your handiwork.

The heavens declare the glory of God.

In Your love You have given us the power
to behold the beauty of Your world,
robed in all its splendor.
The sun and the stars,
the valleys and hills,
the rivers and lakes
all disclose Your presence.

The Earth reveals God's eternal presence.

The roaring breakers of the sea
tell of Your awesome might;
the beasts of the field
and the birds of the air
bespeak Your wondrous will.

Life comes forth by God's creative will.

In Your Goodness You have made us able to hear
the music of the world.
The raging of the winds,

the whisperings of trees in the wood,
and the precious voices of loved ones
reveal to us that You are in our midst.

A divine voice sings through all creation.
—U.N. Environmental Sabbath

Blessed by the Lord be the land,
with the precious gifts of heaven,
with the dew, and the deep that lies beneath,
with the precious fruits
    brought forth by the sun
and the riches
    brought forth by the moon,

with the greatness of the ancient mountains,
with the abundance of the everlasting hills,
and with all the treasures of the earth
    in its perfection.
—Deuteronomy 33: 13–16

O baker of yeast-scented loaves,
sword dancer,
seamstress, weaver of shattering glass,
O whirler of winds, boat-swallower,
germinant seed,
O seasons that sing in our ears in the shape of O—
we name your colors muttonfat, kingfisher, jade,
we name your colors anthracite, orca, growth-tip of pine,
we name them arpeggio, pond,
we name them flickering helix within the cell, burning coal tunnel, blossom of
salt,
we name them roof flashing copper, frost-scent at morning, smoke-singe of
pearl,
from black-flowering to light-flowering we name them,
from barest conception, the almost not thought of, to heaviest matter, we name
them,
from glacier-lit blue to the gold of iguana we name them,
and naming, begin to see,
and seeing, begin to assemble the plain stones of earth.

—Jane Hirshfield

Earth's body is not for sale
or rent. She is real
and we are her estate.
But no body is property.
Not even God owns any of it,
but delights in its being its own.

An ancient forest is always
in a dynamic state, half
of its body actively growing,
half of it actively dying—
these are the same half!

The other half is always
eating and being eaten.
Trees live for two thousand years
and then are food for as long.
This is perpetual and holy communion.

Nobody owns the sacred.
Every body is sacred.
Pray for the future:
become an animal spirited
and glorious in your Earthbody.
Offer thanks when you lie down
with the trees.

—Alla Renée Bozarth

O Sacred Womb of love and grace
We can feel you all around us
We lift our hands to touch and bless you
for we are held and carried in this holy place

Blessed be this womb
where we can move, and dance and dream
Blessed be this womb
that holds us safe and warm within

Blessed be this womb
your wondrous love encircles us
Blessed be this womb
where darkness folds and nurtures us

Blessed be this womb
that feeds our bodies and our souls
Blessed be this womb
where we are called to root and grow

Blessed be this womb
where we can trust and gently learn
Blessed be this womb
where we must struggle, kick and squirm

Blessed be this womb
where life unfolds her mysteries
Blessed be this womb
where our truest self is dancing free

Blessed be this womb
where we're accepted as we are
Blessed be this womb
where we can rest and feel secure.
—Colleen Fulmer

For the fruit of Your womb,
For the bread of our lives,
For Your hands in the earth we adore You;
For the clear-running springs
Flowing up from our hearts,
Mother God, we sing praises before You!
—Gail A. Ricciuti

Slowly, slowly, they return
To the small woodland let alone:
Great trees, outspreading and upright,
Apostles of the living light.

Patient as stars, they build in air
Tier after tier a timbered choir,
Stout beams upholding weightless grace
Of song, a blessing on this place.

They stand in waiting all around,
Uprisings of their native ground,
Downcomings of the distant light;
They are the advent they await.

Receiving sun and giving shade,
Their life's a benefaction made,
And is a benediction said
Over the living and the dead.

In fall their brightened leaves, released,
Fly down the wind, and we are pleased
To walk on radiance, amazed.
O light come down to earth, be praised!
　　　　　　　　　　　　—Wendell Berry

The forest sings God's praises—
the long exhalation of the earth waking from winter
sings God's praises,
and the mosses hear, and the trees,
the trees with their miraculous white leaves,
like angel wings—they hear,
and add their voices
and the pines whisper it,
and the trailing arbutus carries it over the ground
so that all the forest knows,
singing in silence,
who made them in love and joy,
and they stretch to reach Him,
and I feel their singing
   in my hands as I touch them;
   in my eyes as I see them;
   in my feet as I walk among them.
O God, help me to keep listening.
—Bonita Fogg Smith

393

We are the earth.

Earth is stardust–come–to–life, a magic cauldron where the heart of the universe is being formed. In me, the Earth and its creatures find their voices. Through my eyes the stars look back on themselves in wonder. I am the earth. This is my body.

We are the air.

Air is the breath of the Earth, the movement of life, the quick, violent storm, and the slow, caressing breeze. In my breathing, life is received and given back. My breath unites me to all things, to the creatures that make the oxygen, and to the people that share the same breath: yesterday a victim of AIDS; today a soldier in the Middle East; tomorrow, a poor woman in the Third World. I am air. This is my breath.

We are fire.

Fire is the energy of the universe, the source of power and new life. In my thoughts burn the fires of the original eruption of life; in my emotions, lightning flashes; in my love, new life is conceived. I participate in power. I share in the energy of the universe, to keep warm, to fuel my body, to create my relationships. I am fire. This is my power.

We are water.

Water is the womb of the Earth, from which all life is born. The oceans flow through the Earth, bringing abundance; the oceans flow through me, carrying food, recycling waste, expressing emotions. I am water. This is my life.

—Daniel Martin

Emerald
gold
copper and bronze
day by day she turns the ring
of her seasons
winding it
on the fingers
of her land
until
taking a breath of cold air
she disrobes
and then puts on
a gown of purest white
sprinkled with diamonds
in which to dream
of seasons
yet to come
until
taking a breath of warm sun
she awakens
with opalescent rainbows
day by day
she turns the ring
again
to emerald

—Harriet Kofalk

For diamond-studded velvet
Behind a sliver moon
For music of the nightwinds,
A nightingale's sweet tune—
For whispering trees
And darkening peace—
I Thank Thee.

For mountains carved of sea
pearls
For clouds that shroud their
heights
For pristine air like nectar
And ghostly northern lights
For misty vales
And secret dales—
I Thank Thee.

For fiery fuchsia ribbons
That stream across the sky
For opalescent sunsets
And mornings dipped in
dye
For mornings pale
And day's finale—
I Thank Thee.

For scents that herald spring-
time
For lilac-haunted nooks
For violet's purple fragrance
And merry, trickling
brooks—
For little things
That give souls wings—
I Thank Thee.
—Monica Miller

I do not have to go
To Sacred Places
In far-off lands.
The ground I stand on
Is holy.

Here, in this little garden
I tend
My pilgrimage ends.
The wild honeybees
The hummingbird moths
The flickering fireflies at dusk
Are a microcosm
Of the Universe.
Each seed that grows
Each spade of soil
Is full of miracles.

And I toil and sweat
And watch and wonder
And am full of love.
Living in place
In this place.
For truth and beauty
Dwell here.

—Mary de La Valette

Honey, pepper, leaf-green limes
Pagan fruits whose names are rhymes,
Mangoes, breadfruit, ginger-roots,
Granadillas, bamboo-shoots,
Cho-cho, ackees, tangerines,
Lemons, purple Congo-beans,
Sugar, okras, kola-nuts,
Citrons, hairy coconuts,
Fish, tobacco, native hats,
Gold bananas, woven mats,
Plantains, wild-thyme, pallid leeks,
Pigeons with their scarlet beaks,
Oranges and saffron yams,
Baskets, ruby guava jams,
Turtles, goat-skins, cinnamon,
All-spice, conch-shells, golden rum.
Black skins, babel—and the sun
That burns all colors into one.

—Agnes Maxwell-Hall

Bananas ripe and green, and ginger root,
   Cocoa in pods and alligator pears,
      And tangerines and mangoes and grape fruit,
   Fit for the highest prize at parish fairs.

Set in the window, bringing memories
   Of fruit-trees laden by low-singing rills,
And dewy dawns, and mystical blue skies
   In benediction over nun-like hills.

My eyes grew dim, and I could no more gaze;
   A wave of longing through my body swept,
And, hungry for the old familiar ways,
   I turned aside and bowed my head and wept.
                —Claude McKay

You desert, whose ever-shifting sands reflect the
   constant changing in our own lives,
Whose dry heat brings interludes of repose,
Show us the beauty that comes with purity
   and teach us how to simplify our lives.

You mountains, with stone peaks reaching for the heavens,
   who stood here even when the earth was formed,
You, of dizzying heights and ancient age,
Lend us your perspective,
   For our actions now may yet impact the ages to come.

You meadows and grassy hills,
Whose bright fields of wildflowers
    provide unparalleled beauty in our lives,
Provide us with the time to pause and reflect
    on God's artistry and playfulness.

You forests of sturdy oak, hued maple, and ever green,
You home of deer and bear and rabbit and eagle,
    shelter in our play and hostage to our ambitions,
Grant us your maturity,
    and the wisdom to truly know what we do to ourselves.

401

You age-old rainforest, rampant with life's creativity:
Your tangled masses of trees and vines
    embody our interdependent web.
You are diversity incarnate.
Bestow upon us the ability
    to appreciate the interconnectedness of all being.

You ocean of the deep, keeper of earth's last mysteries.
Beneath your ceaseless waves,
    in your quiet and dark womb did life first begin.
Remind us of our beginnings,
    keep us humble against your vastness,
And know that you are truly the water of life.
                                        —Tom Rhodes

Praise to the Breath of Life!
    He rules this world,
    master of all things,
on which all things are based.

Praise, Breath of Life, to your uproar!
    Praise to your thunder!
    Praise to your lightning!
Praise, Breath of Life, for your rain!

When Breath of Life with his thunder
    roars o'er the plants,
    then, pregnant with pollen,
The flowers burst forth in abundance.

When Breath of Life the broad earth
    with rain bedews,
    the cattle exalt:
"We shall have plenty," they say.

The plants converse with this Breath,
    drenched by his moisture:
    "Our life is prolonged,
for you have made us all fragrant."

Breath of Life, do not forsake me.
    You are, indeed, I.
    Like the Embryo of the Waters
I bind you to me that I may live!
                                    —Atharva Veda XI, 4

Praise God in the highest heavens;
   praise him beyond the stars.
Praise him, you bodhisattvas,
   you angels burning with his love.
Praise him in the depths of matter;
   praise him in atomic space.
Praise him, you whirling electrons,
   you unimaginable quarks.
Praise him in lifeless galaxies;
   praise him from the pit of black holes.
Praise him, creatures on all planets,
   inconceivable forms of life.
Let them all praise the Unnamable,
   for he is their source, their home.
He made them in all their beauty
   and the laws by which they exist.
Praise God upon the earth,
   whales and all creatures of the sea,
fire, hail, snow, and frost,
   hurricanes fulfilling his command,
mountains and barren hills,
   fruit trees and cedar forests,
wild animals and tame,
   reptiles, insects, birds,
creatures invisible to the eye
   and tiniest one-celled beings,
rich and poor, powerful

and oppressed, dark-skinned and light-skinned,
men and women alike,
    old and young together.
Let them praise the Unnamable God,
    whose goodness is the breath of life,
who made us in his own image,
    the light that fills heaven and earth.
                —Psalm 148 (version by Stephen Mitchell)

You will go out in joy
and be led forth in peace;
the mountains and hills before you
will burst into song,
and all the trees of the field
will clap their hands.
Instead of the thorn
will grow the cypress,
and instead of briars
will come up the myrtle.
This will be for the glory of the Lord,
for an everlasting sign
which will not be destroyed.
                —Isaiah 55:12–13

. . . I know nothing else but miracles,
Whether I walk the streets of Manhattan,
Or dart my sight over the roofs of houses toward the sky,
Or wade with naked feet along the beach just in the edge of
  the water,
Or stand under trees in the woods,
Or talk by day with any one I love, or sleep in bed at night
  with anyone I love,
Or sit at table at dinner with the rest,
Or look at strangers opposite me riding in the car,
Or watch honey-bees busy around the hive of a summer
  forenoon,
Or animals feeding in the fields,
Or birds, or the wonderfulness of insects in the air,
Or the exquisite delicate thin curve of the new moon in spring.
These with the rest, one and all, are to me miracles,
The whole referring, yet each distinct and in its place.

To me every hour of the light and dark is a miracle,
Every cubic inch of space is a miracle,
Every square yard of the surface of the earth is spread with
  miracles,
Every foot of the interior swarms with miracles.
                              —Walt Whitman

This grand show is eternal.
It is always sunrise somewhere:
the dew is never all dried at once:
a shower is forever falling, vapor is ever rising.
Eternal sunrise, eternal sunset, eternal dawn and gloaming,
on sea and continents and islands, each in its turn,
as the round earth rolls.

—John Muir

INDEX OF FIRST LINES

409

Index of First Lines

410

413

415

Index of First Lines

417

Index of First Lines

PERMISSIONS ACKNOWLEDGMENTS

Part One: Affirmations and Invocations

The Terma Collective. From "The Box, Remembering the Gift."

Václav Havel. From *Letters to Olga,* by Václav Havel. Copyright © 1983 by Václav Havel. Author's preface copyright © 1989 by Václav Havel. Copyright by Rowohlt Taschenbuch Verlag GmbH Reinbek bei Hamburg. Copyright © 1988, 1989 by Paul Wilson. Reprinted by permission of Henry Holt and Co., Inc.

Marianne Williamson. From *A Return to Love.* Copyright © 1992 by Marianne Williamson. Reprinted by permission of HarperCollins Publishers, Inc.

The Terma Collective. From "The Box, Remembering the Gift."

Ted Loder. Excerpted from Ted Loder's book, *Wrestling the Light.* Copyright © 1991 by Lura Media. Reprinted by permission of Lura Media, Inc., San Diego, California.

Ram Dass. Reprinted with permission from Ram Dass and the Omega Institute. Ram Dass's books and audiotapes are available from the Hanuman Foundation, 524 San Anselmo Avenue, #203, San Anselmo, CA 94960.

Allan Millet. "The Homecoming," by Allan Millet. Copyright © 1992. Reprinted by permission of author.

Pat Cane. Reprinted by permission of author.

Anne Hillman. Adapted from: Anne Hillman, *The Dancing Animal Woman— A Celebration of Life.* Bearsville, New York: Bramble Books, 1994. Reprinted by permission of author.

Harriet Kofalk. "Priorities," by Harriet Kofalk. Reprinted by permission of author.

Judy Chicago. Untitled, from *The Dinner Party.* Copyright © 1988 Judy Chicago.

Fran Peavey. "Prayer" from *A Shallow Pool of Time,* by Fran Peavey. Copyright © 1988. Reprinted by permission of New Society Publishers.

Women's Environment and Development Organization. "A Pledge of Allegiance to the Family of Earth," by the Women's Environment and Development Organization. Reprinted by permission of W.E.D.O.

Thomas John Carlisle. "Gratitude for the Earth," by Thomas John Carlisle. Reprinted by permission of United Nations Environment Programme. Copyright © 1992.

Neil Douglas-Klotz. "The Blessings of Earthiness" from *Prayers of the Cosmos: Meditations on the Aramaic Words of Jesus,* by Neil Douglas-Klotz. Copyright © 1990 by Neil Douglas-Klotz. Reprinted by permission of HarperCollins Publishers, Inc.

U.N. Environmental Sabbath. "Litany for Healing the Earth," by U.N. Environmental Sabbath. Used by permission of United Nations Environmental Programme.

Arthur Waskow. Copyright © 1992 by Arthur Waskow from "Retelling the Rainbow." Reprinted by permission. For more information on "Retelling the Rainbow," write the author at 6711 Lincoln Dr., Philadelphia, PA 19119.

Henry Horton. Copyright © 1989, Henry Horton. All rights reserved.

Gautama Buddha. "Loving Kindness" by Gautama Buddha. This version used by permission of United Nations Environmental Programme.

Thich Nhat Hanh. "Meditation for 1995," by Thich Nhat Hanh. Reprinted from *Mindfulness Bell,* Spring 1995, with permission of Parallax Press, Berkeley, California.

Joanna Macy. "The Beings of the Three Times—a Meditation." Reprinted from *World As Lover, World As Self,* by Joanna Macy (1995) with permission of Parallax Press, Berkeley, California.

Gary Snyder. "For the Children" from *Turtle Island,* by Gary Snyder. Copyright © 1974 by Gary Snyder. Reprinted by permission of New Directions Publishing Corp.

Annie Dillard. Excerpt from *Holy the Firm,* by Annie Dillard. Copyright © 1977 by Annie Dillard. Reprinted by permission of HarperCollins Publishers, Inc.

Dale Pendell. Excerpt from "Some Reveries on Poetry as a Spiritual Discipline," by Dale Pendell from *Beneath a Single Moon,* Johnson and Paulenich, eds., Shambala Publications. Copyright © 1991. Reprinted with permission of author.

Part Two: Kinship with All Life

Joseph Bruchac. "Prayer" from *Near the Mountains,* by Joseph Bruchac. White Pine Press. Copyright © 1987.

Mary de La Valette. "The Animals Prayer," by Mary de La Valette. Used by permission of author.

Jamie Sams. "Making Family," by Jamie Sams. Copyright © 1994 by Jamie Sams. Reprinted by permission of HarperCollins Publishers, Inc.

William Stafford. "Later" from *Learning to Live in the World: Earth Poems,* by William Stafford. Copyright © 1994 by Jerry Watson and Laura Apol Obbink, reprinted by permission of Harcourt Brace & Company.

Deena Metzger. "Oh Great Spirit," by Deena Metzger. Used by permission of author.

Joy Harjo. "Eagle Poem" from *In Mad Love and War.* Copyright © 1990 by Joy Harjo, Wesleyan University Press by permission of University Press of New England.

Papago song. From *Papago Indian Religion,* by Ruth Underhill. Copyright © 1946 by Columbia University Press. Reprinted with permission of publisher.

Chickasaw. "They called them Birds," adapted by Gerald Hausman. Reprinted from *Meditations with Animals,* by Gerald Hausman. Copyright © 1986 Bear and Co., P.O. Box 2860, Santa Fe, NM 87504.

Terry Tempest Williams. From *Refuge: An Unnatural of Family and Place,* by Terry Tempest Williams. Copyright © by Terry Tempest Williams. Reprinted by permission of Pantheon Books, a division of Random House.

Sugaware no Michizane. "The Spider," by Sugaware no Michizane, from *Anthology of Japanese Literature,* by Donald Keene, ed. Copyright © 1955 by Grove Press, Inc.

Yaqui. From *American Indian Poetry,* by George Cronyn, ed. Copyright © 1918, 1934, and renewed 1962 by George Cronyn. Reprinted by permission of Ballantine, a division of Random House, Inc.

Anakreon. From *Sappho and the Greek Lyric Poets,* translated by Willis Barnstone. Copyright © 1962, 1967, and 1988 by Willis Barnstone. Reprinted by permission of Schocken Books, published by Pantheon Books, a division of Random House, Inc.

Kwakiutl Women's Prayer. "Prayer to the Sockeye Salmon," from *Religion of the Kwakkiutl Indians,* by Franz Boas. Copyright © 1930 by Columbia University Press. Reprinted with permission of publisher.

Celtic Prayer. *The Little Book of Celtic Blessings,* compiled by Caitlin Matthews, USA. Copyright © 1994 by Element Inc.

William Stafford. "Outside" from *Learning to Live in the World: Earth Poems,* by William Stafford. Copyright © 1994 by Jerry Watson and Laura Apol Obbink, reprinted by permission of Harcourt Brace & Company.

Green Gulch Zen Center. "The Greening of Buddhist Practice." Reprinted by permission of Green Gulch Zen Center.

Sedonia Cahill. "A Food Blessing" from *The Ceremonial Circle,* by Sedonia Cahill and Joshua Halpern. Copyright © 1992 by Sedonia Cahill and Joshua Halpern. Reprinted by permission of Harper-Collins Publishers, Inc.

The Lotus Sutra. From *Scripture of the Lotus Blossom of the Fine Dharma,* translated by Leon Hurvitz. Copyright © 1976 by Columbia University Press. Reprinted with permission of publisher.

Paiakan. *Earth Memory: Sacred Sites— Doorways into Earth Mysteries,* by Paul Devereux, St. Paul, MN, Llewellyn Publications. Copyright © 1992. Reprinted by permission of Foulsham Publishing.

Robert Nye. "A Proper Place" from *Darker Ends*, by Robert Nye. Marion Boyars Publishers, London and New York.

Bill Clarke. "Tree-being," by Bill Clarke. Reprinted by permission of author.

Arthur O. Roberts. "A Prayer at Tree-Planting," by Authur O. Roberts from *Move Over, Elijah: Sermons in Poetry and Prose*. Barclay Press. Copyright © 1967.

Amergin's Charm. "Amergin's Charm," translated by Robert Graves. From *The Alphabet Calendar of Amergin,* by Robert Graves. Reprinted by permission of Carcanet Press Limited.

David Wagoner. "Lost" from *Collected Poems*, by David Wagoner, Indiana University Press, 1976. Reprinted by permission of David Wagoner.

Part Three: The Dark Night of Our Soul

Wendell Berry. From *Sabbaths 1987–90*, by Wendell Berry. Copyright © 1992 Golgonooza Press.

Arthur Waskow. Copyright © 1992 by Arthur Waskow from "Retelling the Rainbow." Reprinted by permission. For more information on "Retelling the Rainbow" write the author at 6711 Lincoln Dr., Philadelphia, PA 19119.

U.N. Environmental Sabbath. "Prayer of Confession." Reprinted by permission of U.N. Environmental Sabbath.

Mark Van Doren. "Psalm 6" from *That Shining Place,* by Mark Van Doren. Copyright © 1969 by Mark Van Doren.

Helvecio Mendes. From *Flowers on Fire* in the Philippines, by Helvecio Mendes. Reprinted by permission of Claretian Publications.

Rabindranath Tagore. "Question" from *Selected Poems: Rabindranath Tagore,* translated by William Radice, Penguin Books, 1985. Copyright © William Radice 1985.

Hildegard of Bingen. Reprinted from *Meditations with Hildegard of Bingen,* by Gabriele Uhlein, Copyright © 1983, Bear & Co., P.O. Box 2860, Santa Fe, NM 87504.

George Ella Lyon. "Inventing Sin" from *Cries of the Spirit,* by George Ella Lyon, Beacon Press, 1991, Marilyn Sewell, ed. Copyright © George Ella Lyon.

Pima Song. Reprinted from the Bureau of American Ethnology #22 (Washington, DC: Smithsonian Institute Press), Page 291, by permission of publisher. Copyright © 1996.

Rabindranath Tagore. "Flying Man" from *Selected Poems: Rabindranath Tagore,* translated by William Radice, Penguin Books, 1985. Copyright © William Radice 1985.

Li Ch'ing Chao. *One Hundred More Poems From The Chinese,* by Kenneth Rexroth. Copyright © 1920 by Kenneth Rexroth. Reprinted by permission of New Directions Publishing Corp.

Crow Song. Reproduced by permission of the American Anthropological Association from *American Anthropologist* 35, 1933. Not for further reproduction.

Wendell Berry. "To Know the Dark" from *Farming: A Handbook*. Copyright ©

1970 by Wendell Berry, reprinted by permission of Harcourt Brace & Company.

Renee Senolges. Used by permission of author.

Mark Van Doren. "Psalm 9" from *That Shining Place,* by Mark Van Doren. Copyright © 1969 by Mark Van Doren.

Theodore Roethke. "In A Dark Time," by Theodore Roethke. Copyright © 1960 by Beatrice Roethke, Administratrix of the Estate of Theodore Roethke. From *The Collected Poems of Theodore Roethke,* by Theodore Roethke. Used by permission of Doubleday, a division of Bantam Doubleday Dell Publishing Group.

A. Powell Davies. From *Great Occasions: Readings for the Celebration of Birth, Coming of Age, Marriage and Death,* by Carl Seaburg, Beacon Press, Boston, 1968. Reprinted by permission of Muriel Davies.

Rainer Maria Rilke. Reprinted by permission of Joanna Macy, from Rainer Maria Rilke, *The Book of Hours,* translated by Joanna Macy and Anita Barrows, Putnam, N.Y., 1996.

Rumi. "The Guest House," from *The Essential Rumi,* translated by Coleman Barks, Threshold Books, RD 4 Box 600, Putney, VT 05346. Copyright © 1995.

Part Four: Prayers for Solidarity and Justice

Arthur Waskow. Copyright © 1992 by Arthur Waskow from "Retelling the Rainbow." Reprinted by permission. For more information on "Retelling the Rainbow," write the author at 6711 Lincoln Dr., Philadelphia, PA 19119.

Iyamide Hazeley. "Women of Courage" from *Daughters of Africa,* by Margaret Bushy. Copyright © 1992 by Margaret Bushy. Reprinted by permission of Pantheon Books, a division of Random House, Inc.

Kerstin Linqvist and Ulla Bardh. Extract from "Accept Our Deep Longing to Live," by Kerstin Lindqvist and Ulla Bardh. Translated from the Swedish and published in "No Longer Strangers : a Resource for Worship" 1988 WCC Publications, WCC, Geneva, Switzerland.

The Terma Collective. From "The Box, Remembering the Gift."

Daniel Martin. Director of International Communities for the renewal of the Earth. Reprinted by permission of author.

Stephen Mitchell. "Psalm 24" from *A Book of Psalms,* by Stephen Mitchell. Copyright © 1993 by Stephen Mitchell. Reprinted by permission of HarperCollins Publishers, Inc.

Patricia Winters. "A Prayer for Conservation," by Patricia Winters from *Celebrating Earth Holy Days.* Reprinted by permission of U.N. Environment Programme.

Robert Aitken. Reprinted from *The Dragon Who Never Sleeps: Verses for Zen Buddhist Practice,* by Robert Aitken (1991) with permission of Parallax Press, Berkeley, California.

Mother Teresa. "Make Us Worthy Lord" from *A Gift For God,* by Mother Teresa.

original source of Winter psalm; it is adapted in the *Birthings and Blessings II* book.)

Zsuzsanna E. Budapest. From *The Holy Book of Women's Mysteries.* Copyright © 1986, Susan B. Anthony Coven No. 1.

Raicho Hiratsuko. Excerpt from "Women's Manifesto," *Return of the Great Goddess.* Ruth Gottstein, Publisher. Copyright © 1988, Volcano Press, P.O. Box 270, Volcano, CA 95689. Phone: (209) 296–3445, (800) 879–9636. Fax: (209) 296–4515.

Robin Morgan. Excerpt from "The Network of the Imaginary Mother" from *Upstairs in the Garden: Poems Selected and New, 1968–1988,* by Robin Morgan. Copyright © 1990 by Robin Morgan. Reprinted by permission of Edite Kroll Literary Agency.

Nancy Rose Meeker. "The Untamed One." Reprinted by permission of author.

Luisah Teish. "Praise and Love to Those Who Seek . . ." from *Carnival of the Spirit,* by Luisah Teish. Copyright © 1994 by Luisah Teish. Reprinted by permission of HarperCollins Publishers, Inc.

Elayne Clift. "I Listen, and My Heart is Breaking" from *Demons Dancing in My Head,* by Elayne Clift, OGN Publications, 1995.

Mary E. Hunt. "Women-Church Proclamation," by Mary E. Hunt. Used by permission of author.

Robin Morgan. "A Women's Creed, The Declaration of the Women's Global Strategies Meeting." Copyright © Robin Morgan, W.E.D.O. Global Strategies Meeting, 1994.

Hattie Gossett. "World View" by from *Presenting . . . Sister No Blues,* by Hattie Gossett. Firebrand Books, Ithaca, NY. Copyright ©1988 by Hattie Gosset.

Mari Evans. "I am a Black Woman" from *Daughters of Africa,* by Mari Evans. Copyright © 1970 by William Morrow. Reprinted by permission of author.

Susan Griffin. "Three Poems for Women" from *Like the Iris of an Eye,* by Susan Griffin. Used by permission of author.

Sumangalamata. Untitled, by Sumangalamata from *Women in Praise of the Sacred,* by Jane Hirschfield. Copyright ©1994 by Jane Hirschfield. Reprinted by permission of HarperCollins Publishers, Inc.

Anonymous. From *Ornaments of Fire, The Worlds Best 101 Short Poems and Fragments,* by Ed Wheeler, ed., Fithian Press, Santa Barbara. Copyright © 1994.

Medical Mission Sisters. From *Woman-Prayer, WomanSong.* Copyright © 1987 by Medical Mission Sisters. Published by Crossroad Publishing, NY.

Desanka Maksimovic. "For All Mary Magdalenes," by Desanka Maksimovic from *Contemporary Yugoslav Poetry,* by Vasa D. Mihailovich, ed. Copyright © University of Iowa Press, 1977.

Mary Mackey. "Grand Jetee" from *The Deer Dance of Eros,* by Mary Mackey, Fjord Press. Copyright © 1987.

Grand Pueblos prayer. "Song for the Newborn," Grand Pueblos prayer from *The American Rhythm,* by Mary Austin. Copyright © 1923, 1930 by Mary Austin. Copyright renewed by Harry P. Mera, Kenneth M. Chapman and Mary C. Wheelwright. Reprinted by permission of Houghton Mifflin Co. All rights reserved.

Lenora Hatathlie Hill. From *Cry, Sacred Ground: Big Mountain USA.* Washington, DC: The Christie Institute, 1988.

Prince Modupe. Excerpt from *I Was A Savage.* Copyright © 1958 by Harcourt Brace & Company and renewed 1985 by Prince Modupe, Paris. Reprinted by permission of publisher.

Arapaho prayer. "Prayer of an Old Man at a Young Man's Change of Name" from *The Arapaho,* by A. L. Kroeber. Courtesy of the American Museum of Natural History.

Coming of Age

Jim Cohn. "The Secret Desire of Fear" from *Grasslands,* by Jim Cohn, Writers and Books Publications. Copyright © 1994. Reprinted by permission of author.

Traditional Gaelic. "Blessing on a Young Person's Leaving Home," from *The Little Book of Celtic Blessings*, compiled by C. Matthews 1994, published in U.S. by Element, Inc.

Mary Mackintosh. "Blessing for Any Friend," by Mary Mackintosh from *The Little Book of Celtic Blessings,* compiled by Caitlin Matthews 1994, published in U.S. by Element, Inc.

Navajo Prayer. "Prayer to the Mountain Spirit," translated by Mary Austin. "Prayer to the Mountain Spirit" first appeared in *Poetry.* Copyright © 1917 The Modern Poetry Association. Reprinted by permission of the editor of *Poetry.*

Alla Renée Bozarth. "Pure Lust, Perfect Bliss—Holy Communion," by Alla Renée Bozarth. Used by permission of author. All inquiries and requests for permission to reprint any portion of the poem must be directed to the author: Alla Renée Bozarth, Wisdom House, 43222 SE Tapp Road, Sandy, Oregon 97055; Tel. 503–668–3119.

Ursula K. LeGuin. "Initiation Song from the Finders Lodge." Copyright © 1985 by Ursula K. LeGuin; first appeared in *Always Coming Home,* Harper and Row, 1985. Reprinted by permission of author and author's agent, Virginia Kidd.

Cormac. From *Selections from Ancient Irish Poetry,* translated by Kuno Myers, Constable & Company, 1913.

Nancy Wood. From *Many Winters,* by Nancy Wood. Copyright © 1974 by Nancy Wood. Illustrations copyright © 1974 by Frank Howell. Reprinted by permission of Bantam Doubleday Dell Books for Young Readers.

Nanao Sakaki. "If you have time to chatter" from *Break the Mirror,* by Nanao Sakaki. Copyright © 1987 by Nanao Sakaki. Reprinted by permission of North Point Press, a division of Farrar, Strauss & Giroux, Inc.

Rainer Maria Rilke. From *Letters to a Young Poet*, by Rainer Maria Rilke, translated by Stephen Mitchell. Copyright © 1984 by Stephen Mitchell. Reprinted by permission of Random House, Inc.

W. S. Merwin. "For the Departure of a Stepson" from *The Rain in the Trees*, by W. S. Merwin, Copyright © 1988 by W. S. Merwin. Reprinted by permission of Alfred A. Knopf, Inc.

Courtship

Anonymous Japanese. From *Ancient Poetry From China, Japan, and India*, translated by Henry W. Wells, Univ. of South Carolina Press, Columbia, 1968.

Judy Grahn. "Paris and Helen" from *The Queen of Wands*, by Judy Grahn. Copyright © 1982 by Judy Grahn, The Crossing Press, Freedom, CA.

Constance Lindsay Skinner. Excerpt from "Summer Dawn," by Constance Lindsay Skinner. "Summer Dawn" first appeared in *Poetry*. Copyright © 1966 the Modern Poetry Association. Reprinted by permission of the editor of *Poetry*.

Constance Lindsay Skinner. Excerpt from "Summer Dawn," by Constance Lindsay Skinner, op.cit.

Nancy Rose Meeker. "Flame of Alchemy" from *Eight Facets of Womanspirit,* by Nancy Rose Meeker. Reprinted by permission of author.

Chippewa Song. "In the Great Night," from *American Indian Poetry*, translated by Frances Densmore. Reprinted from the Bureau of American Ethnology #22

(Washington, DC: Smithsonian Institute Press), pages 22–23, by permission of publisher.

Inca Song. Inca Song, translated by Garcilaso de la Vega from *The Sacred Path,* by John Bierhorst, ed. Copyright © 1983 by John Bierhorst. By permission of Morrow Junior Books, a division of William Morrow & Co., Inc.

Anambe prayer. From *The Sacred Path,* by John Bierhorst, ed. Copyright © 1983 by John Bierhorst. By permission of Morrow Junior Books, a division of William Morrow & Co., Inc.

Ariel and Chana Bloch. From *Song of Songs,* by Ariel and Chana Bloch. Copyright © 1995 by Ariel and Chana Bloch. Reprinted by permission of Random House, Inc.

Emily Dickinson. "Wild Nights" from *Poems by Emily Dickinson*, by Martha Dickinson Bianchi and Alfred Leete Hampson, eds. Little, Brown & Company, Boston, 1950.

Susan Griffin. "Three Love Poems" from *Unremembered Country*. Copyright © 1987 by Susan Griffin. Reprinted by permission of Copper Canyon Press, PO Box 271, Port Townsend, WA 98368.

Simon J. Ortiz. "Watching You" from *Woven Stone*, by Simon J. Ortiz, University of Arizona Press, 1992. Reprinted by permission of author.

Ellen Bass. Excerpt from "Live for It" from *Woman of Power*, by Ellen Bass. Reprinted by permission of author.

Stephen Mitchell. "Psalm 1" is from *A Book of Psalms,* by Stephen Mitchell. Copyright © 1993 by Stephen Mitchell. Reprinted by permission of Harper-Collins Publishers, Inc.

Sappho. "Verse 46" from *Sappho: A New Translation,* Copyright © 1958 The Regents of The University of California; © renewed 1984 Mary Barnard.

Marriage Vows and Blessings

Rumi. From *Love is a Stranger,* by Rumi; translated by Kabir Helminski. Copyright © 1993 Threshold Books, RD 4, Box 600, Putney, VT 05346.

Zsuzsanna E. Budapest. "A Marriage Ceremony for Those Who Feel It is Time for Trysting" from *The Grandmother of Time.* Copyright © 1989 by Zsuzsanna Emese Budapest. Reprinted by permission of HarperCollins Publishers, Inc.

Deena Metzger. "Seven Blessings." Used by permission of author. "Seven Blessings" is the author's broad translation and interpretation of the traditional Hebrew 7 Marriage Blessing.

Fritz Hull. Used by permission of author.

Thich Nhat Hanh. Used by permission of author.

Miriam Therese Winter. "Blessing Song" from *WomanPrayer, WomanSong,* by Miriam Therese Winter. Reprinted by permission of Medical Mission Sisters.

James Bertolino. "A Wedding Toast" from *Graces,* by June Cotner. Used by permission of author.

Atimah. From *Ceremonies of the Heart: Celebrating Lesbian Unions,* by Becky Butler, ed. Seal Press, 1990.

Denise Levertov. "Prayer for Revolutionary Love" from *The Freeing of the Dust.* Copyright © 1975 by Denise Levertov. Reprinted by permission of New Directions Publishing Corporation.

Simon J. Ortiz. "Mid-America Prayer" from *Woven Stone,* by Simon J. Ortiz, University of Arizona Press, 1992. Reprinted by permission of author.

Druidic Vow. "Traditional Druidic Vow" from *The Druid Way,* by Philip Carr-Gomm. Copyright © 1993 by Element, Inc.

Kuan Tao-sheng. "Married Love" from *Woman Poets of China.* Copyright © 1972 by Kenneth Rexroth. Reprinted by permission of New Directions Publishing Corporation.

Carmina Gadelica. "Blessing for a Lover" from *The Little Book of Celtic Blessings,* by Caitlin Matthews. Copyright © 1994 by Element, Inc.

Gaelic Prayer. Excerpt from "Blessing on a Young Person's Leaving Home" from *The Little Book of Celtic Blessings,* by Caitlin Matthews. Copyright © 1994 by Element, Inc.

Norma Woodbridge. "Prayers for Our Home" from *Graces,* by June Cotner. Reprinted by permission of author.

The Siddur of Shir Cadash. From *Ceremonies of the Heart: Celebrating Lesbian Unions,* by Becky Butler, ed. Seal Press, 1990.

430

Navajo Prayer. "Song of Dawn Boy," by Navajo Prayer. Reprinted from the Bureau of American Ethnology #22 (Washington, DC: Smithsonian Institute Press), page 74 by permission of publisher. Copyright © 1996.

Mhairi nic Neill. "Blessing for a Newborn Child" from *The Little Book of Celtic Blessings*, by Caitlin Matthews. Copyright © 1994 by Element, Inc.

Medical Mission Sisters. From *WomanPrayer, WomanSong*, by Medical Mission Sisters. Words by Miriam Therese Winter. Copyright © 1987. Medical Mission Sisters. Reprinted with permission of Medical Mission Sisters.

Midlife

William Butler Yeats. "Vacillation," by William Butler Yeats. Reprinted with the permission of Simon and Schuster from *The Poems of WB Yeats: A New Edition*, by Richard J. Finneran, ed. Copyright © 1933 by Macmillan Publishing Company, renewed 1961 by Bertha Georgie Yeats.

Sharon Olds. "35/10" from *The Dead and the Living*, by Sharon Olds. Copyright © 1983 by Sharon Olds. Reprinted by permission of Alfred A. Knopf Inc.

Gladys May Casely-Hayford, "Aquah Laluah." "To My Mother," by Gladys May Casely-Hayford from *Daughters of Africa* by Margaret Bushy. Copyright © 1992 by Margaret Bushy. Reprinted by permission of Pantheon Books, a Division of Random House, Inc.

Mark Van Doren. "My brother lives too far away" from *Good Morning*, by Mark Van Doren. Copyright © 1973 by the Estate of Mark Van Doren. Reprinted by permission of Hill and Wang, a division of Farrar, Strauss & Giroux, Inc.

Rabbi Rami M. Shapiro. "Morning" from *Tangents*, by Rabbi Rami M. Shapiro. Reprinted by permission of author.

Judith Gass. "Tides of Your Life," by Judith Gass. Used by permission of author.

Fleur Adcock. "Weathering." Copyright © Fleur Adcock 1983. Reprinted from Fleur Adcock's *Selected Poems* (1983), by permission of Oxford University Press.

Mavis Muller. "Agave/I Gave," by Mavis Muller. Reprinted by permission of author.

Dan Gerber. From *Beneath a Single Moon*, by Kent Johnson and Craig Paulenich, eds. Shambala Books, 1991. Reprinted by permission of author.

Pawnee Song. "Song to the Mountains" from "Songs from the Hako." Reprinted from the Bureau of American Ethnology #22 (Washington, DC: Smithsonian Institute Press), page 185 by permission of publisher.

Guatama Buddha. "The Five Remembrances," by Guatama Buddha. Reprinted from *Plum Village Chanting and Recitation Book*, compiled by Thich Nhat Hanh (1996) with permission of Parallax Press, Berkeley, California.

Kabir. From *The Kabir Book,* by Robert Bly. Copyright © 1971, 1977 by Robert

431

Bly. Reprinted by permission of Beacon Press.

Wendell Berry. "Ripening" from *A Part*, by Wendell Berry. Copyright © 1980 by Wendell Berry. Reprinted by North Point Press, a division of Farrar Strauss & Giroux, Inc.

Growing Older

Joseph Bruchac. "Canticle" from *Near the Mountains*, by Joseph Bruchac, White Pine Press, 1987.

Gail A. Ricciuti. *Birthings and Blessings II: More Liberating Worship Services for the Inclusive Church*, by Gail Anderson Ricciuti and Rosemary Catalano Mitchell; Copyright © 1993 by Gail Anderson Ricciuti and Rosemary Catalano Mitchell. Used with permission of The Crossroad Publishing Company, New York.

Robert Terry Weston. From *Dealing Creatively with Death, A Manual of Death Education and Simple Burial*, by Ernest Morgan. NY: Zinn Communications, 1994.

W. S. Merwin. "Snow" from *The Rain in the Trees*, by W. S. Merwin. Copyright © 1988 by W. S. Merwin. Reprinted by permission of Alfred A. Knopf Inc.

Celtic Prayer. From *The Little Book of Celtic Wisdom*, by Caitlin Matthews. Copyright © 1993 by Element, Inc.

Hsin Ch'i Chi. "To an Old Tune" from *One Hundred More Poems from the Chinese*. Copyright © 1970 by Kenneth Rexroth. Reprinted by permission of New Directions Publishing Corporation.

Su Tung-p'o. "Viewing Peonies at the Temple of Good Fortune" from *The Selected Poems of Su Tung-p'o 1994*, by Burton Watson, translator. Reprinted by permission of Copper Canyon Press, P.O. Box 271, Port Townsend, WA 98368.

Saigyo. From *Art, Life and Nature in Japan*, by Masaharu Anesaki, Charles Tuttle Company, Rutland, VT, 1984.

Kiyo. "Zen Poem" from *Zen Poems of China and Japan*, by Lucien Stryk and Takashi Ikemoto, eds. Copyright © 1973 by Lucien Stryk, Takashi Ikemoto and Taigan Takayama.

Kenneth Rexroth. "For Eli Jacobsen" from *Collected Shorter Poems*, by Kenneth Rexroth. Copyright © 1956 by Kenneth Rexroth. Reprinted by permission of New Directions Publishing Corporation.

John Hall Wheelock. "Dear Men and Women," by John Hall Wheelock. Reprinted with the permission of Scribner, an imprint of Simon & Schuster from *Dear Men and Women,* by John Hall Wheelock. Copyright © 1963 John Hall Wheelock. (First appeared in *The New Yorker*, July 1963.)

Susan Griffin. "Born into a World Knowing" from *Unremembered Country*, 1987, by Susan Griffin. Reprinted by permission of Copper Canyon Press, PO Box 271, Port Townsend, WA 98368.

William Stafford. "Four Oak Leaves" from *An Oregon Message*, by William Stafford. Copyright © 1987 by William Stafford. Reprinted by permission of HarperCollins Publishers, Inc.

Ogden Nash. "Old Men" from *Verses from 1929 On*, by Ogden Nash. Copyright © 1931 by Ogden Nash. Reprinted by Little, Brown & Company and Curtis Brown Ltd. Copyright © 1931 by Ogden Nash, renewed. First appeared in *Publishers Weekly*.

Song of the Teton Sioux. From *American Indian Poetry*, by George Cronyn, ed. Copyright © 1918, 1934, and renewed 1962 by George Cronyn. Reprinted by permission of Ballantine Books, a Division of Random House, Inc.

Wendell Berry. "The Wish to Be Generous" from *Farming: A Handbook*. Copyright © 1969 by Wendell Berry, reprinted by permission of Harcourt Brace & Company.

Death

Mary de La Valette. "Sacred Circles," by Mary de La Valette. Used by permission of author.

Aztec Prayer. From *The Sacred Path*, by John Bierhorst, ed. Copyright © 1983 by John Bierhorst. By permission of Morrow Junior Books, a division of William Morrow & Co., Inc.

Lew Sarett. From *Dealing Creatively with Death*, by Ernest Morgan, Zinn Communications. Copyright © 1994.

Nancy Wood. From *Many Winters*, by Nancy Wood. Copyright © 1974 by Nancy Wood. Illustrations copyright © 1974 by Frank Howell. Used by permission of Bantam Doubleday Dell Books for Young Readers.

Kahlil Gibran. From *The Prophet*, by Kahlil Gibran. Copyright © 1923 by Kahlil Gibran and renewed 1951 by Administrators CTA of Kahlil Gibran Estate and Mary G. Gibran. Reprinted by permission of Alfred A. Knopf Inc.

Anne Stevenson. "Birth" from *Reversals*. Copyright © 1969 by Anne Stevenson, Wesleyan University Press by permission of University Press of New England.

Papago. "In the Great Night" from *American Indian Poetry*, by Frances Denmore. Reprinted from the Bureau of American Ethnology #22 (Washington, DC: Smithsonian Institute Press), page 291, by permission of publisher. Copyright © 1996.

Jim Cohn. "Running into Don at the Cascade" from *Grasslands*, by Jim Cohn. Writers & Books Publications copyright © 1994. Reprinted by permission of author.

Edna St. Vincent Millay. "Dirge Without Music" from *Collected Poems*, by Edna St. Vincent Millay, HarperCollins. Copyright © 1928, 1955 by Edna St. Vincent Millay and Norma Millay Ellis. Reprinted by permission of Elizabeth Barnett, literary executor.

Witter Bynner. "Pause" from *Take Away the Darkness*. Copyright © Witter Bynner. By permission of author.

Linda Pastan. "Last Will" from *A Fraction of Darkness*, by Linda Pastan, with the permission of W. W. Norton & Company, Inc. Copyright © 1985 by Linda Pastan.

D. H. Lawrence. "When the Ripe Fruit Falls" from *The Complete Poems of D. H.*

Lawrence, by D. H. Lawrence, edited by V. de Solo Pinto and F .W. Roberts. Copyright © 1964, 1971 by Angelo Ravagli and C. M. Weekley, Executors of the Estate of Frieda Lawrence Ravagli. Used by permission of Viking Penguin, a division of Penguin Books USA Inc.

Marilyn Krysl. "Grandmother," by Marilyn Krysl. Reprinted from *Prairie Schooner,* by permission of the University of Nebraska Press. Copyright © 1987 University of Nebraska Press.

Wendy Smyer Yu. Reprinted by permission of author.

Jewish Prayer. From *Rabbi's Manual.* Copyright © 1988.

Zsuzsanna E. Budapest. "You are Blessed in Mother's Eyes . . ." from *The Goddess in the Bedroom,* by Zsuzsanna E. Budapest. Copyright © 1993 by Zsuzsanna E. Budapest. Reprinted by permission of HarperCollins Publishers, Inc.

Omaha Prayer. From *Omaha Secret Societies,* by R.F. Fortune. Copyright © 1932 by Columbia University Press. Reprinted with permission of the publisher.

Judith Anderson. "Re-member Us" from Judith Anderson's writing about her etching Re-member Us, which appeared in *Return of the Great Goddess,* Burleigh Muten, Shambala, 1994.

Part Seven: Moments of Grace and Illumination

Denise Levertov. "The Avowal" from *Oblique Prayers.* Copyright © 1984 by Denise Levertov. Reprinted by permission of New Directions Publishing Corporation.

Ted Loder. Excerpted from Ted Loder's book, *Guerrillas of Grace.* Copyright © 1984, reprinted by permission of Lura Media, Inc., San Diego, California.

David Whyte. "Enough" from *Where Many Rivers Meet,* by David Whyte, Many Rivers Press. Reprinted by permission of author.

Thich Nhat Hanh. Reprinted from *Present Moment Wonderful Moment: Mindfulness Verses for Daily Living,* by Thich Nhat Hanh (1990) with permission of Parallax Press, Berkeley, California.

Wallace Stevens. "Final Soliloquy of the Interior Paramour" from *The Collected Poems of Wallace Stevens,* by Wallace Stevens, Faber and Faber, London Copyright ©1945. Reprinted by pernmission of the publisher.

Anna Akhmatova. "A Land Not Mine" from *News of the Universe,* Ally Press, 1985. Copyright © translation Jane Kenyon. Reprinted by permission of publisher.

Rumi. "Quietness" from *The Essential Rumi,* translated by Coleman Barks, Threshold Books, RD 4, Box 600, Putney, VT 05346. Reprinted by permission of publisher.

Anne Hillman. Adapted from: Anne Hillman, *The Dancing Animal Woman—A Celebration of Life.* Bearsville, NY: Bramble Books, 1994. Reprinted by permission of author.

Annie Dillard. Excerpt from *Teaching a Stone to Talk,* by Annie Dillard. Copyright © 1982 Annie Dillard. Reprinted by permission of HarperCollins Publishers, Inc.

William Stafford. "Earth Dweller" from *Learning to Live in the World: Earth Poems,* by William Stafford. Copyright © 1994 by Jerry Watson and Laura Apol Obbink, reprinted by permission of Harcourt Brace & Company.

Cass Adams. "The Forest Lies Within Your Own Heart," by Cass Adams. Used by permission of author.

Thich Nhat Hanh. Reprinted from *Touching Peace: Practicing the Art of Mindful Living,* by Thich Nhat Hanh (1992) with permission of Parallax Press, Berkeley, California.

Antonio Machado. "Last Night" reprinted from *Times Alone: Selected Poems of Antonio Machado,* translated by Robert Bly, Wesleyan University Press, Middletown, CT, 1983. Copyright © 1983 by Robert Bly. Reprinted with his permission.

Rainer Maria Rilke. From *The Selected Poetry of Rainer Maria Rilke,* edited and translated by Stephen Mitchell. Copyright © 1982 by Stephen Mitchell. Reprinted by permission of Random House, Inc.

William Stafford. "Time for Serenity, Anyone" from *Even in Quiet Places,* by William Stafford. Copyright © 1996 by the Estate of William Stafford. Reprinted by permission of Confluence Press at Lewis-Clark State College, Lewiston, Idaho.

Shinsho. "Zen Poem" from *Zen Poems of China and Japan,* by Lucien Stryk and Takashi Ikemoto, eds. Copyright © 1973 by Lucien Stryk, Takashi Ikemoto and Taigan Takayama.

James Broughton. "This is it" from *Special Deliveries,* by James Broughton, Broken Moon Press, Seattle. Copyright © 1990. Reprinted by permission of author.

Part Eight: Earth Praises

Homer. Excerpt from "The Hymn to the Earth" from *The Homeric Hymns,* by Homer. Translated by Charles Boer, Spring Publications. Copyright © 1995.

Nancy Wood. From *Many Winters,* by Nancy Wood. Copyright © 1974 by Nancy Wood. Illustrations copyright © 1974 by Frank Howell. Used by permission of Bantam Doubleday Dell Books for Young Readers.

Stephanie Kaza. Used by permission of author.

Kim Oler. Excerpt from "The Blue Green Hills of Earth," by Kim Oler. Reprinted by permission of U.N. Environmental Programme.

Rabbi Rami M. Shapiro. From *Tangents,* by Rabbi Rami M. Shapiro. Copyright © 1988 Rabbi Rami M. Shapiro.

U.N. Environmental Sabbath. "A responsive reading from a Jewish Prayer." Reprinted by permission of U.N. Environmental Programme.

The Bible. Bible quotations unless otherwise noted, are paraphrased from the New Revised Standard Version of the Bible. Copyright © 1989 by the Division

Elizabeth Roberts, Ed.D., and Elias Amidon have been traveling and working together for the past eleven years. They are on the faculty of the Naropa Institute in Boulder, Colorado, where they teach in the Transpersonal Psychology and Environmental Studies departments. They are co-founders of the Institute for Deep Ecology, a school for spiritually engaged activists. Roberts and Amidon are also trained wilderness guides and lead rites-of-passage ceremonies, spiritual retreats, and personal transformation programs across the United States and throughout Europe and Southeast Asia.

For more information about their wilderness quest work and trainings, please write:

The Qalandar School
1314 Eighth Street
Boulder, CO 80302